# AMAZING JELLYFISH

# AMAZING JELLYFISH

*Michael Stavarič* ✦ *Michèle Ganser*

Translated from the German by Oliver Latsch

*Pushkin Children's*

CHAPTER
01

## OUR JOURNEY CONTINUES

Infinite spaces. Infinite knowledge. Infinite ways to tell all about it.

I look up at the night sky and see a few bats silently whizzing by. I'm sure you've seen bats, haven't you? I can clearly make out their silhouettes because they stand out against the full Moon.

I wonder where I should begin this story. After all, I have a lot to tell you about our world, its many oceans, the land, the sky (or rather: space). I want to tell you about all the animals that live there and how everything is connected to everything else (and to us). I also want to write a book that you won't want to put down…

Yikes, I've given myself quite the job!

And, of course, I want to tell you all about jellyfish. At first glance, they may not seem exciting or appealing. But you will be amazed at what these mysterious animals can do.

Now I'm stuck trying to count the bats above me. Actually, maybe it's the same bat every time. It's probably buzzing around up there, secretly having a laugh at my expense. Oh, by the way, that word I used earlier: "silhouettes"? You didn't know it? A silhouette is a clear outline or shape. In French, the word refers to a paper cut-out. In the 18th century, a French finance minister named Étienne de Silhouette decorated the walls of his chateau with cut-outs he had made himself. These were then dubbed *Portraits à la Silhouette.* So he sort of invented the word. Interesting, isn't it? Maybe you can ask your art teacher at school to create some bat silhouettes with you. Even better, you should take this book with you. Perhaps the teacher will want to have a read.

Meanwhile, I'm still searching for suitable words with which to really get this story started. I try imagining what it would feel like to float in the sea like a jellyfish, in the dark, completely weightless, just like a star in the sky.

I wonder what it's like to feel weightless. A jellyfish could definitely explain it to us, if only it could speak. But at least I can read what astronauts say about it—people who were actually in space and got to experience weightlessness there. What an adventure!

Gravity is somehow (at least to me) the very opposite of weightlessness. By the way, gravity was discovered by a guy sitting under an apple tree. He thought that if an apple falls from a tree, it must be because the Earth pulls it down. And that's precisely what happens. All bodies attract each other!

At this point, I can hear a few of you, the particularly smart ones, asking: "Hey, Michael, what else do these bodies attract? A pair of trousers? A blouse? A skirt?" Fine, have a laugh. Of course, I'm not talking about that kind of body. No, this is science, after all. I meant that all the things in the universe attract each other: planets, stars, galaxies. They're like magnets, and the greater a body's mass (which is kind of like its weight), the stronger its gravitational pull. Actually sounds quite logical, doesn't it?

Our Earth, for example, has a greater mass than the Moon (and it is also much larger) so it strongly attracts the Moon, which in fact would cause the Moon to crash into the Earth, if the Moon weren't orbiting us at breakneck speed. Nice of the Moon to do that for us. This is an example of "centrifugal force", like when Mum or Dad drives the car too fast around a bend, and everyone inside is pushed outwards. That's how the Moon feels all the time, it's forever speeding around a bend. Which is good for us, or else it would fall on our heads. I don't know about you, but I prefer my Moon up in the sky so that the bats can flutter around in front of it. Now, let's return to this "gravity" that apparently makes all the things in the universe attract each other. It's what keeps us on Earth—and not floating weightlessly into space. And since there is no switch to turn off gravity on Earth, we can't really experience weightlessness down here. Or can we?

I read about a tower in the German city of Bremen that can simulate weightlessness. Scientists throw different things into a vacuum chamber (which sounds like a great job, by the way), and everything you throw down there becomes weightless for four seconds. Weightlessness can, of course, also be simulated reasonably well underwater. Astronauts often train in water. They are meticulously fitted with different weights until they neither sink down nor float upwards—and *voilà*, they are seemingly weightless. Just like jellyfish, which, by the way, have also been to space. I'll get to that in a moment.

But if you ask me, true weightlessness can only be experienced in space. Many astronauts have described feeling blissfully happy as they float about up there. But "weightlessness" isn't good for humans in the long term, and maybe you can guess why: because your muscles waste away! After all, everything is so easy in space, and you don't have to work so hard with your hands and legs. You keep floating, your muscles weaken, and when you eventually return to Earth, you can't walk properly any more. Then you have to exercise again to build up your muscles. It's a back-breaking job, being an astronaut. And for those who need to know more: it's not only our muscles that suffer in space. Our skeletons need regular vibration, or our bones start to waste away. To stop this happening, astronauts have to spend time standing on "vibration boards". Well, if that's not funny, I don't know what is.

Astronauts also take various animals into space for research and observe them there. So yes, jellyfish have gone to space, as have other terrestrial creatures. If you are interested in this, you can read the section "For Bright Minds" right now—as for the rest of you, just stay here with me.

The explanation of why NASA (the American space agency) is interested in jellyfish initially sounds a bit complicated. Both humans and jellyfish rely on unique gravity-sensitive calcium crystals to orient themselves in space. In humans, these crystals are located in the inner ear; in jellyfish, they are located at the lower edge of their mushroom-shaped bodies. So, basically, jellyfish and humans orient themselves in a similar way, even though they are very different creatures. By the way, the first animals in space were various insects, followed by hamsters, pigs, spiders, water bears (look them up!), fish, fruit flies, mice, dogs, frogs, geckos, monkeys, rabbits, threadworms and butterflies.

## FOR BRIGHT MINDS

Jellyfish have been to space, and not too many of us can say that for our-selves. NASA began repeatedly taking these animals up into orbit back in the 1990s. They wanted to test how the medusae (another word for jelly-fish I'll explain later) coped with weightlessness. The jellyfish (including the "moon jellyfish") reproduced magnificently there, but when their off-spring finally returned to Earth, the scientists discovered that they had big problems with gravity on earth. Future humans who are born in space will probably encounter the same problems!

You may have seen old TV pictures of astronauts bouncing around on the Moon, making great leaps across its surface. That's because the gravity on the Moon is not as strong, and we weigh less there than on Earth. Curious, isn't it? Our Moon weight is roughly one-sixth of what we weigh on our own planet. If that sounds complicated, here's a straightforward example: If you weigh sixty kilograms on Earth, you only weigh about ten kilograms on the Moon.

Suppose you want to work out your Moon weight exactly (and I bet some of you do). In that case, you'd better get out your calculator (or you can use one on any mobile phone). The definitive "how-much-I-actually-weigh-on-the-Moon formula" is: Weight on Earth divided by 9.81 multiplied by 1.622. Wait, I'd better check this with the sixty kilograms. Hold on, I'm almost there. Yay, it works. The result is 9.9204893 kilograms. Very close to 10! Maths isn't that bad after all. If only someone had explained it to me like that in school… Oh yes, of course, you will now have the task of calculating your parents' Moon weight—believe me, they will be pleased with the result.

If you don't want to do the calculations yourself, you can also check out the "Weight on the Moon Calculator" on the internet; you'll find the link at the end of the book on page 134.

And you know what? On the Sun, we would theoretically weigh twenty-eight times as much as on Earth because the Sun's gravity is so strong. Gravity is different in different places across the universe, so you have to do a lot of maths: So with the Sun—wait a minute, 60 kilograms multiplied by 28, oops, that's 1,680 kilograms. Well, I definitely don't want to weigh that much. The heaviest jellyfish in the world (I'll tell you more about it later) weighs about 200 kilograms. So that's how much on the Moon? And on the Sun? (You can find the answer on page 136.)

# Made of plastic, it's NOT fantastic

Has this ever happened to you? You're sitting in the countryside by a river, thinking of nothing much, and suddenly you see a plastic bag or bottle floating by in the water. With some imagination, you could even mistake the plastic bag in the water for a jellyfish. I mean, they really look alike. But think about it! All that plastic ends up in the ocean at some point, where it does a lot of damage to the environment (the animals and us).

Did you know there are billions of tonnes of plastic waste in the oceans? I read that it forms enormous "islands" in some places, vast expanses of plastic in the middle of the sea as far as the eye can see. And believe it or not: these "islands" are now about as big as Germany, Austria, Switzerland, Hungary, Czechia and Slovakia put together! Of course, something so large has got its own name: "The Great Pacific Garbage Patch". Maybe sometime in the distant future, people will even have to live on plastic islands in the sea. Who knows.

By the way, say "Pacific Ocean" out loud. Isn't it funny that the letter "c" is pronounced differently three times? I just happened to notice that. You have to pay attention to even the smallest things in life. And while we're at it—there are five oceans in total. The Pacific is the largest. It's followed by the Atlantic Ocean, the Indian Ocean, the Southern Ocean and the Arctic Ocean. You really need to know these things!

Scientists think there are many more, smaller garbage patches. At least four are known: two in the Atlantic Ocean and one in the Indian Ocean. It is difficult to estimate their actual dimensions because most of the plastic is underwater. I can't understand why all the huge fleets from all the countries in the world aren't immediately setting out to remove all this plastic. I really don't get it.

Although three-quarters of the rubbish in the sea is made up of plastic, we can only estimate how many tonnes that all adds up to. The UN Environment Programme (UNEP) calculates that humanity produces around 300 million tonnes of plastic waste per year. The Covid pandemic alone generated an additional 8.4 million tonnes—mainly in hospitals (face masks also contain plastic). Of all this, an estimated 4.8–12.7 million tonnes ends up in the oceans every year. (The biggest "plastic waste offenders" are currently China, Indonesia, the Philippines, Vietnam and Sri Lanka, but the list is very long.) Let's face it, all those numbers don't really mean much. So let me try it another way. My calculator is always handy: an average horse

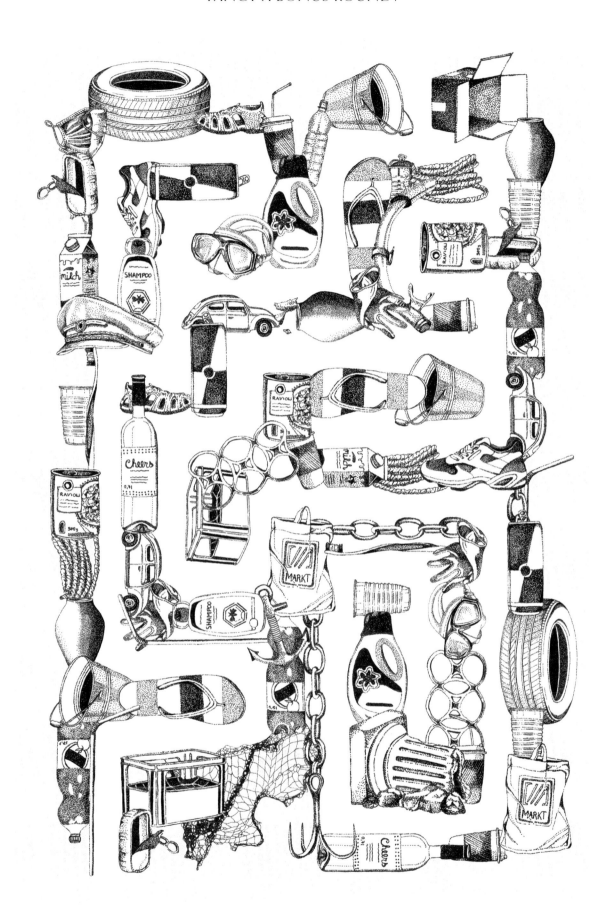

So much plastic... find the way through!

Solution: p. 137

weighs about 500 kilograms. So ten million tonnes of plastic waste would be how many horses? That's a lot, isn't it?

Around 500,000 tonnes of plastic waste from Europe are said to end up in the sea every year—that's pretty much exactly 66,000 rubbish trucks filled to the top. So imagine 66,000 rubbish trucks hauling down to the Mediterranean instead of a landfill. Maybe they go to Italy or the South of France, where we like to go on holiday. And then they dump everything into the water. Plastics can take hundreds, even thousands of years to completely decompose. And until they do, they break down into smaller and smaller particles called "microplastics". These days, when we walk on a beach, it's not just grains of sand we feel under our feet, but many tiny plastic particles too.

These "microparticles" are a problem in the ocean because marine animals mistake them for food. The poor anchovies (which are one of the foundation species of the marine food chain) regularly eat microplastics. These are then eaten by larger fish, and we, in turn, eat those. So the plastic ends up in our bodies too. Exactly what it does there is still a matter of debate among scientists. We don't have enough so-called long-term studies. However, everyone agrees it won't do us any good, especially in ever higher doses. There is talk of cancer, heart disease and infertility.

According to a recent study by the University of Newcastle in Australia, the global average human intake of microplastics is currently up to five grams per week(!)—about the weight of a credit card. Just imagine eating your parents' bank card—fifty-two times a year. That's crazy, isn't it? And all this because lots of people just throw out plastic bottles into the environment. If you ever see people doing that—leaving plastic or any other rubbish in the park or forest or something—you should explain to them that it is not OK. I certainly do!

# FOR BRIGHT MINDS

Anchovies are not stupid, by the way. They mistake all the microplastic in the water for real food because, according to a study in the journal *Proceedings B*, published by the Royal Society, the plastic particles smell like anchovy food. Algae, plankton, and so on attach themselves to these particles, which makes them smell like the food marine creatures usually eat. If a plastic credit card smelt like a pizza, I would probably gobble it up too, if I were hungry enough. Those poor anchovies and their friends!

It is now scientifically confirmed that more than fifty fish and 700 other animal species in the ocean regularly eat plastic. These include sea turtles, which, unfortunately, often mistake larger pieces of plastic for jellyfish.

Jellyfish may actually help eliminate microplastics in the future. Researchers have launched a project called GoJelly, to develop microplastic filters. And to do this, they are thinking of using jellyfish slime, of all things! The GoJelly scientists have discovered that tiny plastic particles stick to the slime, so they think we might be able to add slime to water to filter out the microplastics in it. We can't be sure that this will really work yet, but who knows? Maybe this will be an excellent way to clean up the oceans. And wouldn't it be great if, in the end, the jellyfish helped us to rid all the oceans of microplastics?

It was only recently scientifically confirmed that the seabed is also heavily contaminated with plastic. The deep sea is becoming a repository for plastic waste, says researcher Angelika Brandt from the Senckenberg Research Institute. Thirteen samples were taken at seven locations in the Western Pacific Kuril-Kamchatka Trench, at depths of between 5,740 and 9,450 metres. That is really deep—deeper than Mount Everest is high, and that's the biggest mountain in the world, at 8,849 metres. Anyway, none of the samples were free of microplastics, and they contained a total of fourteen different types of plastic. Isn't it crazy that the deepest parts of the oceans, indeed the entire seabed, are becoming a plastic waste dump?

But microplastics don't just come from rubbish breaking down in the ocean. They are also caused by the abrasion (or scuffing) of plastic materials, such as car tyres (which get rubbed off on the roads) or the washing of synthetic textiles (which are mostly made of polyester). In these ways microplastics can get into rivers and seas, and from there to our water supply.

And now get this: I learnt that even on the most remote hiking trails in the mountains, there are plenty of invisible microplastics on plants and stones, because of the abrasion of our synthetic (plastic) hiking clothing. Perhaps it would make more sense not to buy any synthetic clothing at all, but only things made of wool or cotton. Check your clothing labels: synthetic fibres are hidden behind terms like polyester, polyamide, poly-acrylic and nylon. You should definitely take a look. Let's head for our wardrobes!

# FOR BRIGHT MINDS

Synthetic fibre is made from coal, crude oil or natural gas, and about 70 per cent of all textile fibres produced worldwide are made from these synthetic materials. This is not good because these so-called "fossil fuels" will only last another 100 years or so, according to the most optimistic forecasts. There are lots of other things around us that are made from petroleum. A few examples: shampoo, detergent, soap, hairspray, tooth-brushes, car seats, floors, buckets, foils, mattresses, computer casings, paint, window frames, and so on. Even many medicines like aspirin are made of thirty-five per cent petroleum! Fortunately, many people are now thinking about replacing plastic altogether. Sugar cane plantations, for example (although plantations themselves are often problematic!) produce a lot of fibrous residues, which are then used to make "bioplastic bags" and disposable plates. Mushrooms can also be used to create an alternative form of packaging called "mycelium". You can even make sustainable leather from it. Isn't that cool? Even milk can be used to create a plastic alternative—which you can eat! And maize, too. And algae can be used to make many things, including a substance very similar to the plastics we know. Maybe that's the solution?

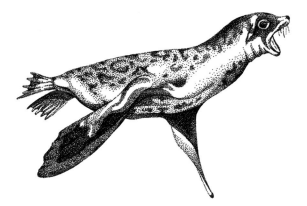

Can you find all seven things that
do not belong in the sea? Solution: p.140

# Jellyfish, Medusae & Co.

I remember the first time I thought seriously about jellyfish. It was when my mum was teaching me how to draw animals. You probably know from your own experience that some animals are relatively easy to draw on paper, and others are really complicated. Jellyfish were the first creatures I learnt to draw as a child because they can be scrawled down really quickly. You make a small semicircle and scribble an infinite number of tangled threads on the bottom, colour everything in—and you have yourself a medusa. Yep, you read that right, "medusa" is what scientists call jellyfish. Maybe because it makes them sound more mysterious.

Would you like to quickly sketch some jellyfish? There's some space for it on this page, and if you want to do it really nicely, then check out the tutorial on the internet (you'll find the link on page 134) that I looked up for you. I swear, had the internet been around when I was a child, I would have drawn much better jellyfish.

Draw more fish, jellyfish or anything
you want in here.

I'm sure some of you have heard of the terrible Medusa, one of Greek mythology's most famous and feared characters. You know, the woman with millions of snakes on her head instead of hair. Everyone who looks her in the eye is immediately turned to stone. Yes, that's the one. In Greek, Medusa's name actually means "guardian". As you can see, there is a lot to say about medusae.

And it's not only jellyfish that bear Medusa's name. No, it appears elsewhere in our human world too: for example, the mysterious Medusa Nebula, which is located high up in space, in the constellation of Gemini. It owes its name to its snake-like gas threads, which reminded astronomers of Medusa's hair.

Apart from that, there are bands, songs, rollercoasters, asteroids, sculptures, mountains (Medusa Peak in Antarctica), lakes, ships, novels, computer programs and so on, all named after the mythical woman. There's even a type of chilli pepper called Medusa. Funnily enough, this pepper tastes sweet and has no heat. Mmm, I'd like to taste that now. And of course, let's not forget a colleague of mine who is a writer and goes by the name of Mieze Medusa. She will be quite amazed when she reads her name in this book.

## FOR BRIGHT MINDS

Medusa has two sisters (Stheno and Euryale). They are all children of the sea gods Keto and Phorkys. They are usually depicted in pictures as winged women with fangs, claws and belts of snakes. According to the Latin poet Ovid, our Medusa has the added problem that she was cursed, by a goddess called Minerva. That's when she got that snake hair, and the power to turn anyone who looked into her eyes to stone. Minerva was the goddess of wisdom. I don't know if it was all that wise to curse Medusa, but who am I to question the gods? The young hero Perseus was charged with killing Medusa. Other gods helped him: he received a dagger and sandals with wings that enabled him to fly. He even got a magic helmet that made him invisible. And the most important thing of all was a shield so shiny he eventually used it like a mirror to defeat Medusa (it worked because he never looked directly at her). I don't know. I always felt sorry for Medusa somehow. Putting a curse on someone is just not right. And it's understandable that, being cursed, your attitude towards your fellow human beings might suffer a bit, isn't it? You should not wish evil on anyone. That sort of thing only creates new monsters.

# The attack of the Australian Medusa

I know you're probably expecting a hair-raising story about how I battled a gorgon, but no. I'll stick to the honest truth. I'm not going to talk about mythical creatures any more. No, from now on, we'll deal with the real medusae, the many jellyfish in the oceans. No jellyfish has ever done anything to me personally. Still, I know a few people who have had quite unpleasant encounters with them. Many medusae are highly poisonous. I'll explain in more detail later how these animals secrete their poison. For now, just remember that there are many toxic jellyfish species, and you should always be on your guard against them when you're in the sea.

Many years ago, I drove through Australia by car along the entire coast, from the north to the south. Since Australia is a whole continent, it took quite a while. On top of that, I drove with the steering wheel on the wrong side! In Europe, cars have the steering wheel on the left (and you drive on the right side of the road). In Australia, Thailand, the UK (which is also kind of Europe, even if it has left the European Union) and other countries, cars have the steering wheel on the right (and you drive on the left side of the road). I never understood why this was so. It can't have anything to do with logic.

So, anyway, I'm sitting behind the wheel of my rental car and driving to the nearest beach. I step out of the vehicle. There's not a soul in sight, and the beach is vast. You can't imagine how big it is. The whole of Australia is kind of a beach when I think about it. The sea is warm, and the waves seem inviting, but then I see it: a warning sign. It looks really menacing. I read the following sentence: "*Marine stingers are present in these waters during the summer months.*"

I must confess that English is not my native language. Still, I understood there was something to watch out for when bathing there. I looked up "marine stingers" in the dictionary. I already knew the word stinger from insects—bees and wasps, for example. I learnt that there are plenty of stinging plants, as well (check out the "suicide plant", *Dendrocnide moroides*!). And soon enough, I learnt about marine stingers, too: the different types of jellyfish to which the warning sign referred. These are mainly "box jellyfish": the Irukandji (*Carukia barnesi*), and the sea wasp (*Chironex fleckeri*).

Funny name, jellyfish. The word jellyfish comes from the nouns "jelly", from the Latin word "*gelare*" meaning "congeal or stiffen", and "fish", which has origins in the Proto-Indo-European word "*pisk*" meaning a "fish, animal that lives in the water". So, literally translated, a jellyfish is a "congealed fish". Isn't that funny? You can congeal water, too, when you freeze

MARINE STINGERS
ARE PRESENT
IN THESE WATERS
DURING SUMMER
MONTHS

it. So the jellyfish is almost like "frozen", or shall we say "congealed" water? I will come back to this later.

Anyway… the sign also said something about pouring vinegar on your skin if you come into contact with one of these jellyfish. And there really were vinegar bottles all over the Australian beaches as first aid in case of an accident with one of the medusae. I was used to dressing my salad with vinegar, but now this?

The poisons of some jellyfish species are among the strongest in the animal kingdom, and vinegar is a semi-reliable remedy that stops the poison cells, the so-called "cnidocytes", of the jellyfish from bursting and thus prevents the poison from escaping. We will talk about this in more detail later, but think about it like this: even when you leave the water, the jellyfish's tentacles continue to stick to your skin and release venom until you pour vinegar on them. Of course, the vinegar doesn't help against the poison already in your body, so if stung by a marine stinger you should also go to a hospital immediately. But it does prevent the stinging cells from pumping more venom into your body.

Some scientists, however, advise against using vinegar. To be safe, pour water at 45 degrees Celsius over the wounds, which will also neutralise the poison. Where you are supposed to

Get very close to the picture until you go cross-eyed. Then slowly pull away!

find 45-degree water on a beach is a mystery. We'll be dealing with jellyfish toxins several more times in this book.

And it just occurred to me—do you distinguish between "stinging" and "biting" as precisely as I do? Many adults don't. Oh, those adults! Jellyfish sting (and release venom), snakes bite (and release venom), lions bite (and don't release venom), Komodo dragons bite (and release venom), and ticks don't bite but sting. So it's strange that we always talk about tick bites. It should really be "tick stings". Some animals sting AND bite. Bumblebees can theoretically do that (but they are very, very peaceful).

A little task for you at this point: Which of these animals sting, which
bite and which can do both? (You can find the answer on page 136.)

1. **Stingray**
- ○ stings
- ○ bites

2. **Horsefly**
- ○ stings
- ○ bites

3. **Hedgehog**
- ○ stings
- ○ bites

4. **Platypus**
- ○ stings
- ○ bites

5. **Thorny devil**
- ○ stings
- ○ bites

6. **Ant**
- ○ stings
- ○ bites

7. **Puffer fish**
- ○ stings
- ○ bites

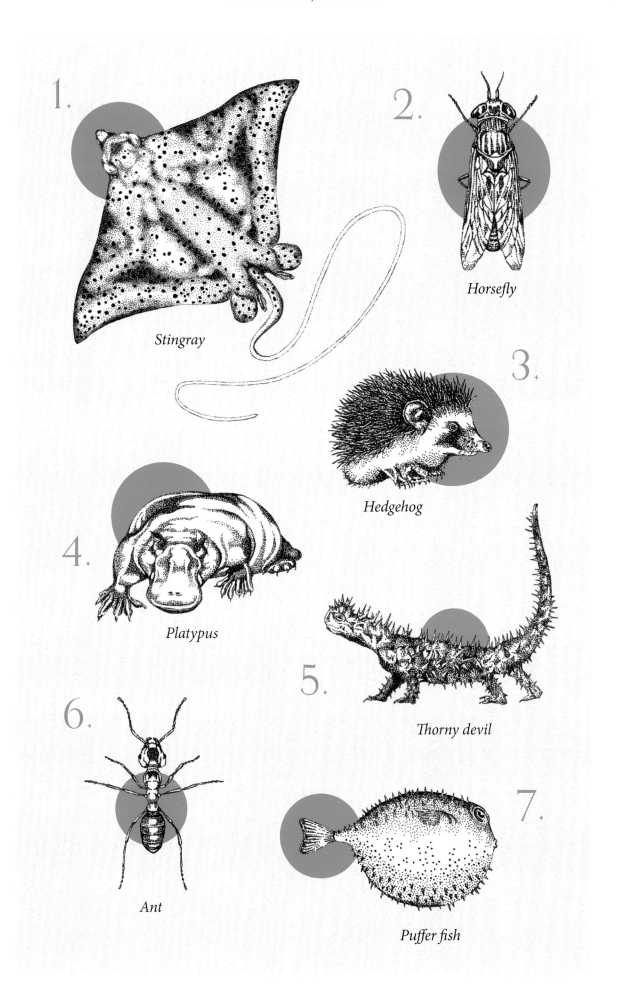

1. Stingray

2. Horsefly

3. Hedgehog

4. Platypus

5. Thorny devil

6. Ant

7. Puffer fish

CHAPTER
✦02

# THE (ALLEGED) TRICKS
# OF THE STINGING NETTLE

When I read about stinger plants in Australia, I immediately thought of the stinging nettle we all know. There must be a lot of stinging nettle species in the world. Wait a minute. I'll quickly look it up. Oh yes, here it is, for those of you who need to know it all: there are about seventy species of stinging nettle, and they belong to the wider nettle family, of which there are about 2,600 species worldwide.

I suddenly realized what it must feel like to come into contact with one of the poisonous medusae: like rolling around in a patch of stinging nettles. Your skin reddens and starts to burn—it's all quite unpleasant. But still, that's nothing compared to the most poisonous jellyfish, which can be deadly. As far as I know, no one has ever died from stinging nettles.

The painful (and itchy) swellings after contact with stinging nettles are caused by their so-called "stinging hairs". The plants have these because they protect them from herbivores. What deer would want to nibble on those? By the way, these stinging hairs are mainly on the upper side of the leaves—so you can safely touch nettles from below.

You have to imagine these stinging hairs like tiny glass tubes that break very easily, creating a point as sharp as a syringe.

This then penetrates our skin, and the stinging nettle poison starts to work. The poison consists of different substances, even formic acid, which we know from ants. There is a lot of advice on the internet about what helps with nettle stings, such as sticking adhesive tape on your skin and pulling it off again. I think rinsing with water, not scratching for ten minutes, and not panicking is quite sufficient.

Nettles don't just sting, though—they are medicinal plants, too. They contain many helpful substances—so please never pull them out of the ground! Where they grow, the soil is always excellent, and butterfly caterpillars love nettles too—more than fifty species live on them, including the map butterfly, the peacock butterfly, the red admiral and the small tortoiseshell. Don't butterflies have the best names? Do you have a favourite butterfly? Every halfway normal person should have a favourite butterfly. That goes without saying. Mine is the "Old World swallowtail". If you don't already have one, I suggest you pick one right away—maybe the "small heath"? Or the "hermit"? Or the "clouded buff"? By the way, around 180,000 butterfly species have been discovered worldwide, so you have a lot to choose from!

Want to know more? On page 134, you'll find a link to native butterflies (with pictures) that you should be able to spot in your garden and out walking. I can do it—so can you! Plus, you'll be able to really impress the adults on your next ramble.

I remember when I was a kid and went fishing with my uncle. At one point, we had to make our way through lots of plants on the bank of a river, and you guessed it, suddenly, there were nettles everywhere! I was pretty scared when I touched them because I didn't know plants could cause such pain. At first, I thought I had been bitten by a mosquito or pricked by some hidden rosehip bushes. But this felt different, and my uncle explained how nettles work.

He didn't tell me about the most dangerous nettle species in the world. Of course, he probably had no idea about that. But we will now: It is the… little drum roll… Australian stinging tree, the "suicide plant" I mentioned earlier. What a surprise. Its scientific name is "*Dendrocnide moroides*", and some Aboriginal Australians (and probably other Australians) call it "gympie-gympie". Even the faintest contact causes hellish pain, which only peaks after half an hour. Dr Marina Hurley from the University of New South Wales describes it this way: "Being stung is the worst kind of pain you can imagine—like being burnt with hot acid and electrocuted at the same time."

I'd love to tell you more (and in detail!) about the world's most dangerous plant species, but that would take us too far away from our jellyfish. Maybe I'll write a separate book about them one day. Shall I? For now, beware of the fruits and flowers of the yew and deadly nightshade, the mandrake and the meadow saffron. And the most poisonous tree in the world is the *manzanilla de la muerte*, which means "little apple of death". We call it the manchineel tree (*Hippomane mancinella*). You would never think of eating "apples of death", would you? The curious thing about this tree is that it secretes a dripping sap that causes severe burns when you stand under it during a rainstorm. Even touching the trunk causes burn-like wounds. And if it catches fire, it produces poisonous gases that cause blindness. Geez! We'll definitely stay away from that one.

Anyway, let's get back to the Cnidaria—our stinging animals! Their scientific name comes from the Greek *knidē* —"nettle". Yes, there is an interesting connection here.

But one thing is true: touching a poisonous jellyfish is a million times worse than walking naked through a patch of stinging nettles. But why would anyone want to walk stark naked through a patch of stinging nettles in the first place? Um, you'll really have to ask them that.

# FOR BRIGHT MINDS
## AUSTRALIA'S MOST POISONOUS ANIMALS

Australia is home to so many poisonous animals (more than anywhere else in the world) because the land is dry and barren. The so-called "outback" is a hard place to survive in, so predators must make sure that every attack is successful. Otherwise they'd starve to death! Oh, and the plants don't want to be eaten either. That's why Australia is definitely the most poisonous continent on our planet.

## 1.
## INLAND TAIPAN

The inland taipan is not just the most poisonous snake in Australia, but probably in the whole world. And that's some claim to fame. Compared to this deadly reptile,

cobras seem like mere earthworms. The species was discovered in 1879 and given the scientific name *Oxyuranus microlepidotus*. The first part of its name, *Oxyuranus*, means "sharp tail" and its species name, *microlepidotus*, translates to "small scales". Small-scaled sharp-tail is a pretty cool name!

Today, the animal is Australia's best-known snake and fascinates people worldwide. It's also known as the fierce snake (for obvious reasons), and the *dandarabilla* to Aboriginal Australians. Its venom consists of a powerful neurotoxin called taipoxin, which stops blood clotting and destroys red blood cells and muscle tissue. The venom from a single bite could kill up to 250 adult humans, 150,000 rats or 250,000 mice. But did you know we extract substances from snake venom to use as medicine? Fascinating, isn't it?

# 2.
## SYDNEY
## FUNNEL
## WEB SPIDER

When I was in Sydney, I was warned about this spider. Venomous spiders are usually found in the wild, but this one lives exclusively in or near to the city of Sydney (to a radius of about 160 kilometres). The females can get as big as the palm of your hand, so they're quite something. They like to spin webs that look like funnels. Many people encounter them while gardening and get bitten on their hands and feet. Their venom is strong enough to paralyse your heart, as well as the muscles you use for breathing.

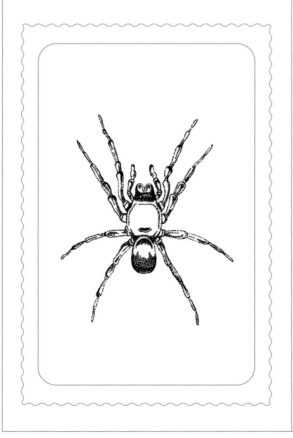

# 3.
## REDBACK
## SPIDER

The redback spider (*Latrodectus hasselti*), also native to Sydney (and indeed all of Australia) is a tough customer. Some people also call it "the Australian black widow" (the "black widow" is another poisonous spider species). Its venom, alpha-latrotoxin, causes cramps and pain that are described as unbearable and last for about twelve hours. If no paralysis occurs in the lungs, there is no immediate danger to life. The males are not poisonous. You only need to watch out for the females. With the help of us humans, these animals also travel far and wide, due to international trade. For example, there is now a new redback spider population in Japan. Researchers have also discovered a natural weapon against the redback spider. The previously forgotten "Captain Cook's wasp" attacks these dangerous animals. First, the wasp paralyses its victim with a sting and then lays an egg in the spider. After the larva hatches, it literally eats the spider from the inside. Phew, poor spider!

# 4.
# BULLDOG ANT

Bulldog ants are widespread in Australia and are considered highly aggressive. *The Guinness Book of Records* considers the bulldog ant the "most dangerous ant in the world", but of course, this is debatable. The venom of the bulldog ant is capable of causing severe allergic shock, potentially killing an adult human. According to one study in Tasmania (part of Australia), 2.7 per cent of the population had been bitten by bulldog ants. One per cent of those bitten had a life-threatening anaphylactic shock (allergic reaction of the body). Australians also describe them as fearless and aggressive, and their size of up to thirty millimetres is impressive. The little animals also have crazy good eyesight and a venomous sting, a frightening combination. Anyone who is stung should cool the wound immediately. The most effective countermeasure has proven to be the injection of adrenaline, which eases the effects of the allergic reaction. However, the most painful ant bite in the world is that of the South American bullet ant. It is equivalent to a gunshot wound and lasts about twenty-four hours. A scientist once described it: "It's like having huge nails driven through your feet and having to walk over red-hot charcoal for a whole day (and night)."

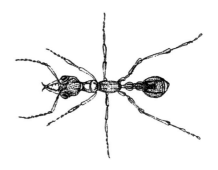

# 5.
# STONEFISH

Have you heard of a "stonefish"? It's super dangerous, primarily due to its unmatched camouflage. It is found on the warmer north coast of Australia, where it lurks almost invisible and motionless, waiting for its prey. If it gets close enough to smaller fish, it sucks them in. Fish with a big mouth like to do that. If you open your mouth underwater, you create a vacuum—and everything in the vicinity is sucked in. The stonefish carries thirteen poisonous spines on its back. It uses them exclusively for defence. For us humans, it is dangerous because it can hardly be distinguished from a stone in the water. A sting leads to severe pain at the puncture site, followed by paralysis and later death. The recommended first-aid measures against the nerve poison are to remove the stingers and to immerse the wound in hot water. Australian doctors also inject an antidote made from the blood of horses, but around sixty per cent of stings are fatal.

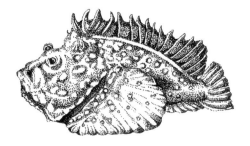

# 6.

## SEA WASP

I already mentioned the sea wasp, known to scientists as "*Chironex fleckeri*". It lives near the Pacific beaches of northern Australia, and its venom is terrifying. I'd better tell you right away that the sea wasp doesn't look like a wasp. We will meet it again later in this book. For now, I'll just say this: the venom of the sea wasp causes incredible pain if you are touched by its tentacles. Your skin and muscles start to decompose, the venom attacks the heart muscle through the bloodstream as well as damaging blood vessels and red blood cells, which can lead to a heart attack. Due to the arrangement of the stinging cells on the tentacles, the victims are left with characteristic "rope ladder patterns" that are burnt into the skin. Death can occur within a few minutes without emergency medical treatment. The sea wasp is often considered the most poisonous marine animal in the world, and many people die from its venom every year. Shark attacks are nothing compared to this.

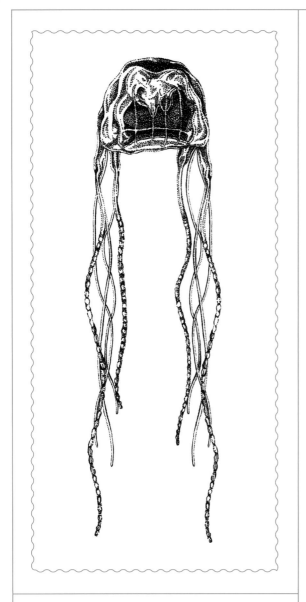

Europe are lucky in comparison. It's called the Australian paralysis tick. Most ticks cause diseases by releasing viruses and bacteria into the bloodstream. This one adds its own toxin to the mix, which can trigger paralysis. The paralysis tick has killed more people in Australia than any other arachnid. The first symptoms only appear after twenty-four hours. First, you feel a tingling in your face, hands and feet. Later you experience paralysis and balance problems. Finally, the respiratory muscles fail, which will kill you.

# 7.

## TICK

Worldwide, there are about 900 species of ticks. In the UK alone, about twenty-two. Phew, I mean, who likes ticks? Many species transmit diseases such as TBE (tick-borne encephalitis), Lyme disease or babesiosis. The east coast of Australia is home to the most poisonous tick species in the world, so we in

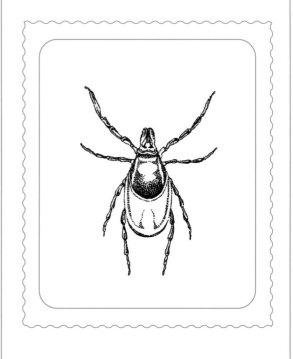

# What is this Michael actually good at?

In the first book in this series (*Amazing Octopus*), I told my readers all the things I wanted to be when I was a child—from an astronaut to a writer to a marine biologist (you can read about it there!). In this book, I would like to tell you a bit more about myself, so that we can get to know each other a little better. OK then: what can I do reasonably well, and what are some other interesting facts about me?

1. This may not interest you, but my favourite number is seven. As a child, I read an adventure book called *Black Seven,* which I loved. I was also born on 7th January. In my experience, everyone secretly has a favourite number. What is yours? And why?

   I have read that people whose favourite number is seven supposedly have the following characteristics: they are studious, sensitive, intelligent, discreet, reliable, helpful and compassionate. On the negative side, they are over-sensitive, arrogant, reclusive, and give up quickly. Well. Of course, I don't quite believe any of that. After all, when it comes to claims and opinions like that, in books and on the internet, anyone can say anything. It's not really science.

More interesting is the fact that some numbers crop up more frequently in the history of mankind. Just think about it: There are the seven seas, the seven deadly sins, the seven wonders of the ancient world, there are seven days in a week, and according to the Bible, the creation of the world only took seven days. The Jewish menorah has seven arms for seven candles, the famous writer Dante describes seven circles of hell, and Babylonian temples always had seven levels. And we would all like to be in the proverbial "seventh heaven", wouldn't we? And that's just for starters—I could give plenty more examples.

2. I was born in Czechoslovakia, so Czech is my mother tongue. Do you know the cities of Prague and Brno? I was born in Brno, and I loved visiting Prague. It was also there that I first read the motto of my homeland. You can find it on the Czech president's flag (actually, it's called a standard, not a flag): *Pravda vítězí*! Truth prevails! That sounds nice, but when did truth ever actually prevail? And if so, which truth?

The most famous tongue-twister that all children learn in Czech is *Strč prst skrz krk*, or, 'put your finger through your throat'! Well, it doesn't make sense, but Czech doesn't need vowels (a, e, i, o, u) to form words. That's curious, isn't it?

3. I love to travel—not only to Australia! I have been to so many countries that listing them all would take quite a while. For example, I remember riding an elephant through the Thai jungle for several days. In China, I went down the Li River on a wobbly raft. In the Seychelles, I saw dragon blood trees and fairy terns. And those tall buildings in New York that the planes flew into? I went there too. At some point, life becomes nothing but memories, just wait and see!

4. I love to swim. I'd love to swim around the world, but I'm not fit enough. Besides, I can only swim breaststroke, and to take on a challenge like that you should at least be able to do front crawl and backstroke. And I absolutely cannot dive! I feel all weird if my head goes underwater. Maybe that's because I can never open my eyes underwater. I bet you can, right?

5. I like to collect things that catch my attention in some way. Nothing in particular. It could be anything: old postcards, feathers, paintings, records, tin cans, music boxes, kaleidoscopes (those are great!), hats, stones, plants (which I press in books to dry), porcelain figurines, shells, whatever. I then imagine what these things

have already experienced, everywhere they've been, who held them in their hands before me and what those people liked about them. In this way, I feel I am "time-travelling", at least into the past.

By the way, you could theoretically travel into the future. A physicist once explained this to me. You would only have to fly near enough to a black hole (do you know about those objects in space?) because time passes much more slowly there than it does here. Then, if you travelled back to Earth after a while, many years would have passed here, while you would barely have aged—you'd be in the future! In the meantime, people on Earth would have invented new technology and would live very differently, so you would seem like a traveller from the past to them. Strange to think about, isn't it?

6. I would love to be able to talk with animals. I've wished I could do it ever since I was a child. I wonder what I'd hear if I could understand them? Maybe something like: Hey, dude, watch it with your giant slippers! (Ant). Do you like my milk, baby? (Cow). Kiss me, kiss me! (Frog). What do you think animals would say to us? Maybe you could send me your thoughts? You will find a way to contact me at the end of this book.

7. And finally, a fact that is not totally silly, considering the subject of this book: I like to go to zoos and look at all the animals there, especially those in aquariums. I sometimes visit the House of the Sea in Vienna. The North Sea Oceanarium in Hirtshals, Denmark, is excellent— it's the hugest aquarium I've ever seen, and it's home to the biggest moonfish you can imagine. But my favourite thing is standing in front of jellyfish tanks and watching them go round and round. There's something magical about it, and seeing them relaxes me a lot. Jellyfish are truly mysterious beauties.

According to a study in 2015, scientists from the University of Plymouth found that being near fish, jellyfish and other sea creatures enhances our health and well-being. Blood pressure dropped significantly in the people they tested, and their heart rate slowed down. At the same time, their mood improved. The study also proved for the first time why so many dentists' waiting rooms have aquariums.

CHAPTER
03

✦

# IMMORTALITY

Have you ever heard of Frankenstein's monster? It's featured in countless movies. You won't be able to avoid watching at least a few of them in your lifetime. The author Mary Shelley "invented" it. She wrote a book called *Frankenstein; or, The Modern Prometheus*. This book is about bringing a dead person, or someone put together from different parts of dead people, back to life. Should you succeed in doing that (and in the book, it works), that would be tantamount to immortality (eternal life). After all, how could someone who had already died once ever die again?

People have dreamt of immortality since the beginning of time. We are already living much longer today than in the past. But some scientists would like to prolong our lives even further. At first glance, that sounds very good.

Ancient and even more recent cultures—you know, Egyptians, Aztecs, Vikings and so on—always hoped for eternal life in a realm "beyond" (they all had different names for it, of course), where they would be united with their gods forever. In our times, many people believe in heaven, a paradise, or something like that. Some place where they can continue to exist after death. And you know what? I don't think it would be a bad idea if we all met again somewhere after death—and chatted and laughed together.

Science would like to give us that immortality here on Earth. People are already being frozen after death to be woken up later when science has worked out how to do it. Scientists are also thinking about stopping the process of ageing by repairing and replacing everything that breaks down in our bodies over time. A bit like we can do with cars. And just as a side note, the oldest person in the world was a woman who lived to the age of 122.

Our bodies can actually repair themselves. At least, they can do so for a long time—but at some point, they lose this ability, which scientists call "resilience". This is the body's ability to regenerate itself. According to science, this resilience disappears entirely after 120 to 150 years. So that is the longest you could possibly live, before you have to die.

I have read a lot about ageing, immortality and so on, and to sum up: no one seriously believes that humans will one day be immortal. What may become a reality is that we can all live in perfect health without problems for about 120 years. That's not bad, either!

# 7 TIMES FUN

~~~~~~~~~

1. What did Sherlock Homes say when investigating the mystery of the murdered jellyfish? Jellymentary, my dear Watson.

2. What do you call a jellyfish in a boat? A stringy thingy in a dinghy.

3. We're on a beach. One tourist asks another: Do they have jellyfish here? The other answers: No, of course not. The sharks ate them all.

4. Who wears a pink tutu and swims in the ocean? A jellerina.

5. Two little jellyfish spot their first submarine. Don't worry, says their mum, those are just canned humans.

6. How do jellyfish like to fly? In a jellycopter.

7. What's a jellyfish's favourite sightseeing spot in London? Jellyphant and Castle, of course.

~~~~~~~~~

# So, how come there are immortal jellyfish?

Yep, that's right—there are immortal jellyfish! How cool is that? I was writing about the impossibility of human immortality. Meanwhile, this animal can theoretically live forever, until the end of time. A genuine superhero!

It won't surprise you that this medusa is one of my favourite jellyfish species (I'll tell you about my other favourites later). It is one of the most exciting animals on our planet because the immortality thing is something no one else has worked out. Some say that sea anemones can live forever, but the *Turritopsis dohrnii* (which is the scientific name of the immortal jellyfish) is clearly the brightest star in the "immortality heavens".

Since this jellyfish species was discovered, scientists have meticulously studied the animal to discover its secrets. This medusa is really tiny, just three to five millimetres in size. It was first discovered in the Mediterranean Sea but has now been found in practically every ocean and seems to thrive in all of them.

The Japanese biologist Shin Kubota has worked out a lot about the "immortal jellyfish" in his laboratory in Kyoto. He has cracked how this immortality thing actually works. It's like a butterfly changing back into a caterpillar, then hatching again, flying around for a while, living a happy butterfly life and switching back into a caterpillar—and on and on. I can't explain it any plainer than that.

In the case of medusae, they change back into so-called "polyps" (we'll talk later about how jellyfish bodies work and how they actually reproduce). Think of polyps as tiny plants—they actually look like little palm trees. They are firmly anchored to the sea floor like coral. Mr Kubota proved that the jellyfish "age back" into their initial polyp form. They do this, for example, when they are stressed, and they can rejuvenate themselves as often as needed. In his laboratory, he documented the process fourteen times; in the wild, this process has been shown to continue forever.

Imagine if we could do the same thing as these jellyfish—be born, grow up, live for a while and then turn back into babies. Then grow up again and go on forever. That would be cool, of course. But I'm not sure if it's really as great as it sounds at first. For example, would you want to go to school over and over again forever? Or have to get your driving licence over and over again? Or get married again and again? Exactly!

And we must be clear that the "immortal jellyfish" is immortal, but it is also someone's food. If it gets eaten, then its immortality is over. Anything that small is hunted practically all the time. And on top of that, this species of jellyfish is cannibalistic. In other words, they also eat each other. That sounds pretty stressful.

All jellyfish bodies are up to ninety-nine per cent water (more about that later). When they wash up on the beach and die, they evaporate within a few hours and disappear completely. Kind of a magic trick, isn't it?

# FOR BRIGHT MINDS

It is a fact (and quite an alarming one) that jellyfish can multiply extremely quickly. Many scientists call this process a "jellyfish bloom". Algal blooms are when there is too much algae in the water. You've probably seen it somewhere before. Jellyfish and algal blooms have already reached dangerous proportions in many areas. On the coast of Israel, not long ago, jellyfish clogged up the intake pipes of a desalination plant which turns salty seawater into drinking water. Jellyfish also once took out a power plant in the Philippines when they were sucked into its cooling pipes. And in Japan, jellyfish have caused fishing boats to sink by getting caught in the nets, which become so heavy that the boats capsize. A huge swarm of jellyfish even attacked a salmon farm and killed 100,000 fish. Some scientists want to use air bubbles to keep jellyfish away from fish farms.

Others are developing submersible robots that cut up cnidarians (yikes!). There are even attempts to predict these giant swarms with the help of computers (like a weather forecast). The so-called slipper cone jelly (*Beroe cucumis*) is known to eat other jellyfish. So when there was a plague of other jellyfish species in the Black Sea in the 1980s, these animals were quickly released. Surprisingly, it actually worked.

With global warming, as our seas warm and become more acidic, jellyfish populations are expected to increase, especially since populations of their predators such as sharks, tuna, turtles and seals are set to decline. I have even read predictions by pessimistic scientists that the last animals in the oceans will be jellyfish. In other words, the oceans will be overflowing with jellyfish—and it will be the fault of humankind, like everything else that's going wrong in this world.

# Let's get on with it– my favourite medusae!

My seven personal favourite medusae are presented for your consideration. These are the ones I'd love to see in an aquarium (see page 70 for illustrations):

1. Of course, I love the longest jellyfish in the world because it makes quite a statement. This breath-taking animal has a diameter of up to three metres. Its 12,000 tentacles can grow up to thirty-six metres long (they also never get tangled because they are slippery). Wow! That makes this medusa bigger than the mightiest animal in the world, the blue whale. It goes by the beautiful name of the lion's mane jellyfish (*Cyanea capillata*), but it is also called the red jellyfish. The famous fictional detective Sherlock Holmes once investigated a death caused by injuries from one of these jellyfish in "The Adventure of the Lion's Mane", by Sir Arthur Conan Doyle. You may want to read it. It's a thrilling detective story!

2. The Portuguese man o'war (*Physalia physalis*) is undoubt-
edly one of the most beautiful, impressive and deadly animals in the sea. It is also known as "the floating terror".
With the words "war" and "terror" in its name, there are
no prizes for guessing that this is a dangerous jellyfish.
It's classified as a siphonophore, a type of colonial hydro-
zoan (I may tell you more about these at another point).
That basically means the Portuguese man o'war consists
of many individual organisms that have joined together
to form a colony (a bit like a large residential community). It usually floats on the surface of the water (thanks
to a gas bladder) which has also earned it the nickname
"bluebottle" or "*botella azul*". In case of danger, it can
empty this gas bladder—and dive down very quickly. In
Australia alone, thousands of people are stung by this
jellyfish species every year. The stings cause excruciat-
ing pain and can even lead to death. Nevertheless, some
animals, such as loggerhead sea turtles or moonfish, eat
these jellyfish and consider them delicacies. They must
be immune to the poison.

3. The Irukandji. That's a strange name for a jellyfish, isn't it? The scientific term "*Carukia barnesi*" is named after the Australian doctor Jack Barnes, who came across these medusae in the 1960s. The word "Irukandji" derives from an Aboriginal people who originally lived on Queensland's north-east coast. The members of this tribe conversed in a language called "Yirrgay". They called themselves the "Yirrganydji". This became the word "Irukandji", and that's how we can also pinpoint the location of the animals geographically. Doctors have a term to describe the terrible effects of being stung by these jellyfish: "Irukandji syndrome". The symptoms include pretty much every unpleasant pain you can think of: intense headaches, agonizing backaches, muscle pains, devilish chest and stomach pains, nausea, vomiting, sweating, heart palpitations, etc. The Irukandji jellyfish is only two centimetres long, so it's tiny and easy to overlook in the water. It also appears on television from time to time. In the American series *Blacklist*, this jellyfish was used to torture people. The TV series *1000 Ways to Die* showed the case of an American student who once accidentally swallowed one of these jellyfish. They numbered it 389 of 1,000 ways to die. But somehow, that kind of list seems in bad taste, doesn't it?

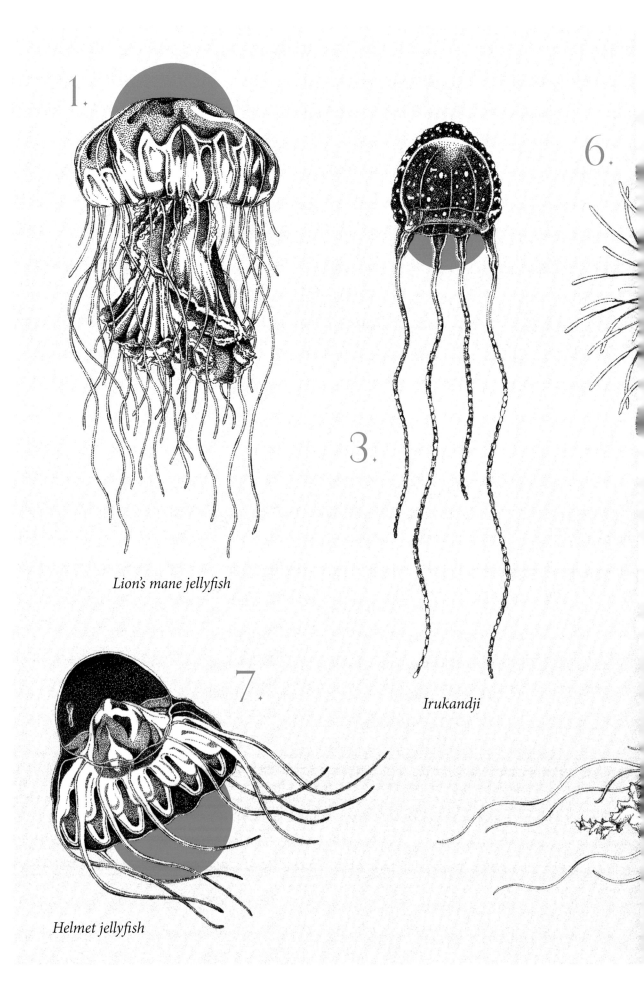

1.

*Lion's mane jellyfish*

3.

*Irukandji*

6.

7.

*Helmet jellyfish*

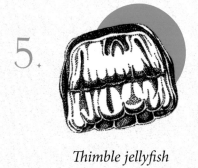

5.

*Thimble jellyfish*

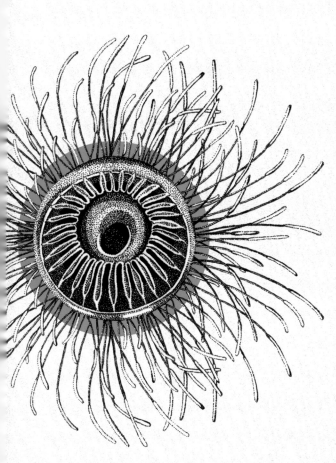

*Firework jellyfish*

4.

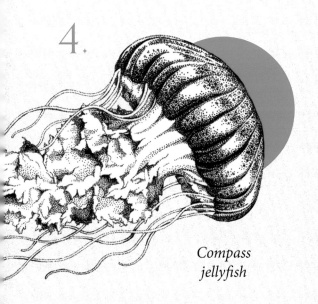

*Compass
jellyfish*

2.

*Portuguese man o' war*

4. Compass jellyfish are much more easy-going than Irukandjis, but that doesn't mean you can safely touch them. At two metres long, at least they're hard to miss. And if you get stung, it "only" hurts like a bee sting. Well, more like a load of bee stings, because jellyfish sting several times. It all depends on how much skin contact there is. Scientific literature says that these medusae are only very rarely fatal. That's almost reassuring, considering how many deadly jellyfish species are out there. Compass jellyfish, by the way, live in the Mediterranean and the North Sea as well. So I'm much more likely to run into them than the others listed here. Sometimes they wash up on the beach in large numbers. Watch where you step! The compass jellyfish is a hermaphrodite—it starts out as male, later becomes simultaneously male and female, and even later becomes female only. Cool, isn't it? It owes its name to its characteristic markings reminiscent of a compass. You know, the little thing that helps you figure out north, south, east, west. Some of the grown-ups you know probably have a compass on their mobile phone—you should have them explain it to you!

5. The thimble jellyfish: Do you know what thimbles are? I loved playing with them as a child. There were always some in my grandma's sewing basket. You put them on your fingertips to sew without pricking yourself with the sharp needle. You can find very beautiful, decorated thimbles—and some people even collect them as a hobby. However, I am convinced that none of them have ever heard of the thimble jellyfish, "*Linuche aquila*". Given its name, you won't be surprised to learn that it is a small medusa. It grows to a maximum of sixteen millimetres long and thirteen millimetres high, so it's a real pip-squeak. Maybe that's why it likes to form large swarms, which can be as big as 1,000,000 m2. How many football pitches is that? (A standard football pitch is 7,140 m2).

The thimble jellyfish's microscopic larvae offspring (I'll tell you more about them soon), can cause a condition called "seabather's eruption". They sometimes get caught in swimming trunks and swimming costumes, and when the swimmer leaves the water and showers, the larvae cause a severe, itchy rash on their skin—only on the parts of their body covered by their swimwear. It looks bizarre. Imagine you had a sunburn, but only on your bum! For a long time we had no idea what caused it, but today we know that the offspring of the thimble jellyfish are responsible for seabather's eruption.

6. The firework jellyfish: This medusa is definitely one of my favourite jellyfish. After all, it looks like real fireworks. It was discovered in 1909, but it is only now that we get to take truly spectacular pictures of it, made possible by modern diving robots with their spotlights and cameras. The firework jellyfish lives at a depth of about 1,500 metres in the Gulf of Mexico. So, unfortunately, you will never see it under normal circumstances. Its scientific name is *Halitrephes maasi*, and when you shine a light on it, it really does glow in every conceivable neon colour. Its 300 tentacles create a natural light show as it swirls around in the current. You really must watch some of the videos on the internet. Sadly not much else is known about this animal, which is true of many jellyfish species. I can't even tell you if it's poisonous. It's high time new generations of explorers (oh yes, I'm talking to you!) set out to learn more about the deep sea and its creatures.

7. Helmet jellyfish live in the fjords of Norway and in the Mediterranean Sea. They are not a rare species. Their population has increased in the last forty years, especially in Scandinavia, which is problematic for the whole ecosystem. The helmet jellyfish, like all jellyfish species, is a successful hunter. If there are too many of them, they will eat all the food of larger fish. The effects on the fishing industry are serious. Indeed, this jellyfish has long been displacing other sea creatures. Strangely, they seem to be able to reproduce and survive even when their food stocks are running low. Marine biologists are currently investigating the cause. My guess is cannibalism! The helmet jellyfish grows up to thirty centimetres, is reddish in colour and produces its own light through bioluminescence (you can read more about this in *Amazing Octopus*). It seems certain that these jellyfish communicate with each other via light signals. The helmet jellyfish feels at home in waters up to seven kilometres deep, almost the height of Mount Everest. At that depth, the water pressure is such that every square centimetre of its small body bears a weight of about one tonne! Crazy, isn't it? It leaves the depths at night and swims upwards to eat its fill.

CHAPTER
04

# MEDUSAE 101

Let's talk about medusae in general and learn some basics about the jellyfish world: their body structure, habits, animal classes, age, etc.

I found an interesting term that some scientists use to express how they think about jellyfish—they call them "organized water". Confused? Well, put it like this. Here is a (theoretical) recipe for a medusa: Take one litre of water and dissolve about eight to fifty grams of salt in it. Add about ten grams of organic components, like amino acids, proteins and carbohydrates. Then allow this mixture to solidify (we already discussed this in explaining the word "jellyfish"!) to form a jelly-like mass. From this, you shape the umbrella and tentacles. Well, that's it for our jellyfish. All that's left to do is to breathe life into it somehow.

Now, this jellyfish you've made actually consists of ninety-four to ninety-nine per cent (!) water (so no solid components like bones, cartilage and so on). Up to five per cent of its body is salt, and less than one per cent is made up of those "organic" components. If you think about it, medusae really are just water that has somehow organized itself into a life form.

This is fascinating because jellyfish exist as organisms. They are alive, like you and me and all other animals. But they don't have a brain or need a heart or lungs, and under their umbrella is only a stomach and mouth (the mouth is also their anus). Nevertheless, they float through water like graceful fairies, so beautiful that you can hardly take your eyes off them. Medusae catch their prey (mainly small fish and crustaceans) with their numerous tentacles (where the infamous nettle cells, or "cnidocytes", are found). As soon as they touch something in the water, these cells shoot countless tiny harpoons (if you don't know what these are, just imagine tiny needles) full of poison. This paralyses the prey, and the jellyfish can digest it in peace.

It's high time to look at a medusa in cross-section. That will give you a much better idea of the animal.

The biological structure of medusae is not rocket science. As you can see, they have an outer and inner skin. The latter is mainly there to line the stomach. In between is a slimy layer, the strange "mesogloea". And no, I can't really pronounce that either!

For those of you who need to know everything: "*Mésos*" means "middle" in Greek, "*ho gloios*" means "sticky oil"—so right in the middle of the sticky oil or something like that.

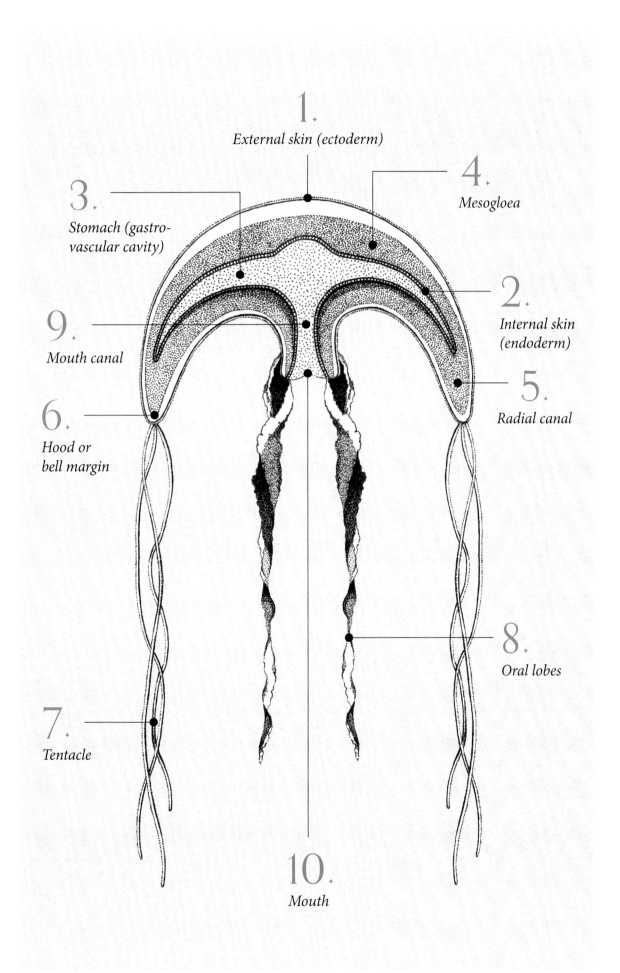

1.
External skin (ectoderm)

4.
Mesogloea

3.
Stomach (gastro-
vascular cavity)

2.
Internal skin
(endoderm)

9.
Mouth canal

5.
Radial canal

6.
Hood or
bell margin

8.
Oral lobes

7.
Tentacle

10.
Mouth

# Help the jellyfish find the right food!

Solution: p. 138

In jellyfish, this mass is responsible for buoyancy in the water. Very important!

Numerous channels lead from the stomach to the umbrella's edge, where the medusa's sensory cells are located. They are so sensitive that they can directly process all signals from the environment (that's why jellyfish don't need a brain). They also perceive gravity and light, for example. Their skin is so thin that they can absorb oxygen from the water directly (that's why they don't need lungs). Finally, the tentacles with the poisonous and dangerous cnidocytes are at the umbrella's edge. And then there are the "oral arms", with which the jellyfish transports its food to where the mouth is located. Well, that's it! Of course, there are precise scientific names for everything, but we'll spare ourselves those now.

I find it particularly exciting that jellyfish have existed for at least 500 million years. That's a whole eternity before the dinosaurs showed up. The great mystery is how they managed to survive on this planet despite all the disasters that have wiped other creatures out.

By the way, what we call a jellyfish is only one of several stages in this animal's life cycle. Just like the butterfly goes through a caterpillar stage, and the frog starts out as a tadpole. Only

after that do the actual creatures we are familiar with emerge. Oh yes, and jellyfish are, as already mentioned, "cnidarians". Corals and anemones are also cnidarians.

## So how are jellyfish really made?

First, the female jellyfish lays many eggs, which are fertilized by the males (or vice versa: the males release their sperm, and the females lay their eggs after, which works too!). Later, tiny larvae hatch (just like insects). These swim around in the open water and eventually settle on the seabed. There they turn into… small drum roll… "polyps".

By the way, if a fish bites off a large piece of a jellyfish polyp, the polyp can regenerate itself completely—it grows back immediately. This is a kind of "superpower" jellyfish possess at this point in their lives. And sure, plants can do that too, of course, but they're not animals!

Anyway, here it comes… medium drum roll… a polyp does not immediately develop into a jellyfish. Instead, it becomes a "polyp 2.0" that biologists call "strobila".

# FOR BRIGHT MINDS

The smart ones among you will want to know more, so here's the scientific definition: in zoology, "strobilation" is a type of asexual reproduction by a spontaneous constriction into body segments. I didn't understand that either, but it will become more evident in the following paragraphs.

These "constrictions" and "divisions" into new segments give rise to the so-called "ephyra". Trust me, I had never heard all these words before and had to look up many things in clever books to find out precisely what they meant. In any case, the "ephyra" is another new larval stage of the jellyfish, from which…

Oh, that's enough now. You know what? Pictures speak louder than words.

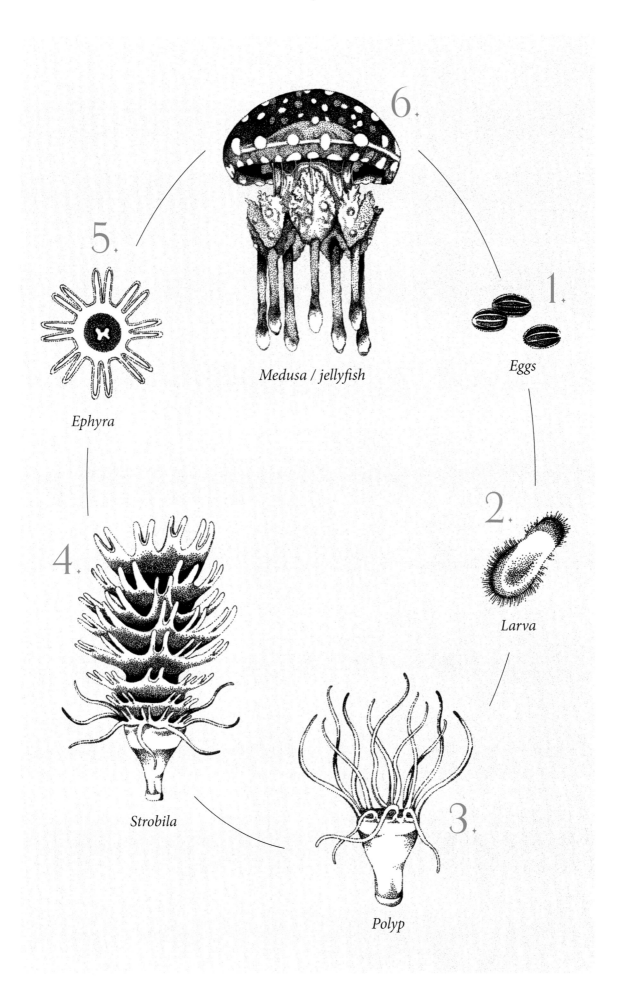

6.

Medusa / jellyfish

1.

Eggs

5.

Ephyra

2.

Larva

4.

Strobila

3.

Polyp

The ephyra is an "almost jellyfish" already floating around in the sea (it looks like a disc-shaped UFO). It quickly grows into the animal that we know as the medusa. It's not all that complicated, is it? I almost forgot: under water, you can't talk about UFOs (unidentified flying objects). Here, unknown objects are called USOs (unidentified swimming objects).

Speaking of jellyfish "superpowers", we should definitely mention the biggest jellyfish (by umbrella size!) in the world: the Japanese Nomura's jellyfish (*Nemopilema nomurai*). They are several metres long and can weigh a good 200 kilograms.

The longest tentacles (up to forty metres) are those of the lion's mane jellyfish, which I have already told you about.

The smallest medusae, on the other hand, have an umbrella half a millimetre wide, which makes them practically invisible in the water. And just imagine the juveniles of these mini jellyfish species. They really are the tiniest specks of dust. Is being as small as a speck of dust actually a superpower?

How long do medusae usually live? That's relatively easy to answer—even though there are several correct answers. Apart from the particular case of the "immortal jellyfish", most medusae live from a few hours to several months. Some even live for a year (like the "moon jelly"), but only a few can live even longer (up to a few years).

## Classes of jellyfish

No, jellyfish don't have to go to school. Zoology groups various creatures into "classes" and "orders", "families" and "genera", and so on. This makes things more straightforward and easier to understand. For example, lions, tigers, leopards, lynx, ocelots, etc., belong to the cat family (from the order "carnivores").

Similarly, there are many different species of jellyfish, although not everything is as clear-cut as with cats. Cats have been studied way more than jellyfish. Many species of jellyfish are also still completely unknown. Sometimes, even science has a hard time classifying these animals because it is unclear which belongs where. Imagine there was a cat that looked almost like a dachshund. It would have the build and coat of a dachshund and eat, walk and behave like a dachshund. Hmm, in that case wouldn't it be more "correct" at first to

speak of a dachshund 2.0 rather than a cat? Anyway, we will now learn about one of these zoological "orders" together. After that, we'll be done with all the jellyfish theory and we can sit back and relax!

The cnidarians (nettle animals, i.e. those that are part of the jellyfish family) are split into groups as follows:

1. True jellyfish (Scyphozoa): These are also called disc or lobe jellyfish, and we currently know about 200 species. Most of them float freely in the water, but there are also "weirder" types, such as the "upside-down jellyfish", which anchors itself to the seabed and points its tentacles towards the sunlight. So it's a jellyfish that constantly stands on its head. Not bad! Sometimes they even carry crabs on their backs. Gymnastic exercises with crustaceans. It keeps getting better and better.

   What about you? Can you do a headstand?

2. Box jellyfish (Cubozoa): We know of about thirty species of these. Their umbrella forms a square bell, with bundles of tentacles dangling from the corners. This

jellyfish family has real eyes! The highly dangerous sea wasp belongs to this class of animals. You have already met it earlier in this book.

3. **Stalked jellyfish** (Staurozoa): These are also called "cup jellyfish". They have a stalk that expands into a cup-shaped top. And they often attach themselves to rocks like corals. They are a bit like those "upside-down jelly-fish" from before but look much more like flowers. Give your grown-ups flowers sometimes, you'll make them happy!

4. **Colony jellyfish** (Physaliidae): Also known as sipho-nophores, these animals form colonies like some insect species (see page 102). In these colonies, the individual animals always specialize in something, such as digestive processes or defence against enemies. The most famous of the resulting colony organisms is the Portuguese man o'war, which we have already met.

5. **By-the-wind sailor** and **blue button jelly** (Porpitidae): The former are also organized in colonies, consisting of

many specialized polyps. They can form swarms several kilometres long and are considered harmless to humans. The latter are usually small animals and look like blue, yellow or green flowers floating on the water's surface. They should not be confused with algae.

6. **Comb jellies** (Ctenophora): These are not really cnidarians. They look as much like real jellyfish as two peas in a pod (think of the "dachshund cat"), but they do not have poisonous cnidocysts. One species (*Haeckelia*) steals the venom of other cnidarians by eating them. This almost makes it like a real cnidarian—clever, right? The red tortuga is particularly beautiful because of its colour, which sets it apart from many other see-through species. There's also a type of snake called the Tortuga Island diamond rattlesnake, which slithers around on Tortuga Island in the Gulf of California, but that's another story.

There is a comb jellyfish species in the North Sea called the sea gooseberry (*Pleurobrachia pileus*). I'd be interested in that one too. Oh yes, colony jellyfish, by-the-wind sailors, blue button jellies and comb jellyfish are collectively known as hydromedusae. A total of about 800 species are known.

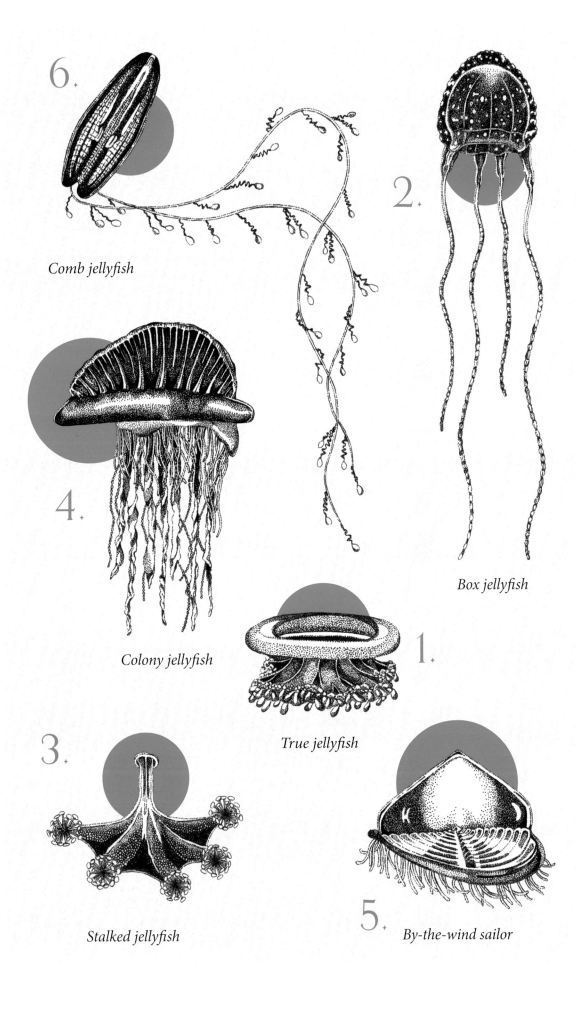

6.

Comb jellyfish

2.

Box jellyfish

4.

Colony jellyfish

1.

True jellyfish

3.

Stalked jellyfish

5.

By-the-wind sailor

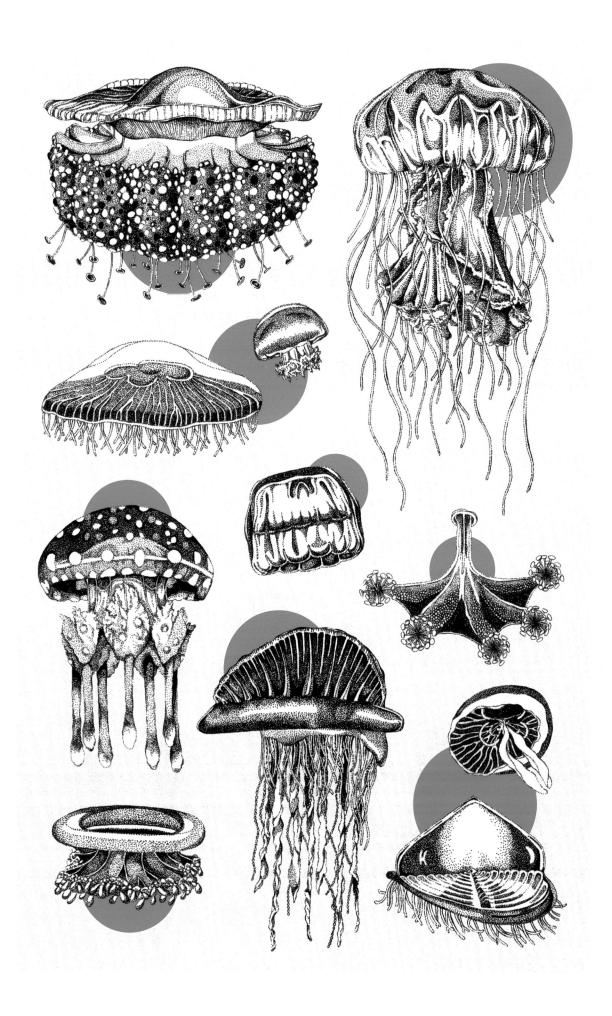

# FOR BRIGHT MINDS

Scientists are very interested in medusae. Jellyfish proteins can be used to help reveal the structure of human cells, so we can examine them better. Some researchers are even trying to develop a type of biocollagen from jellyfish. Collagen is the most common protein in the human body. Thirty per cent of our protein is collagen. It is a substance that lends strength to many parts of the body. In combination with human cells, biocollagen can be used to regenerate joint cartilage—for example, for people suffering from arthritis. Some face creams also contain jellyfish collagen.

Are there any freshwater jellyfish? Oh yes, of course! Even near me, in Vienna, on the Old Danube, and in the UK, where they were spotted in the Shropshire Union Canal. Freshwater jellyfish are harmless and only appear when the water quality is good. Their generic name is *Craspedacusta*. Sounds like a crunchy chocolate bar, if you ask me. The jellyfish species is called *Craspedacusta sowerbii*, and you can only see it once a year when it gets very hot. This species has the highest water content recorded in an animal: 99.3 per cent. Unfortunately, I have never seen these medusae with my own eyes. But I will definitely go on a jellyfish expedition next summer. Who is coming with me?

CHAPTER

05

# CAN JELLYFISH
# FORM NATIONS?

Do you know what the UN is? It is the abbreviation for one of the most famous organizations in the world, the United Nations. Basically, it's a place where all (or almost all) countries meet regularly to discuss problems. I think they should talk more about microplastics, endangered species, environmental protection, and so on, but nobody asks me.

The headquarters of the United Nations is in New York. Maybe you live in New York, or have been there, or if not, maybe you will do one day. I really liked the city, but that's not what I want to tell you here.

In 2021, the UN projected images of sea creatures onto the walls of its headquarters to draw attention to rising sea levels, extreme weather and biodiversity loss. You know, climate change! And the sea creatures they chose to project were siphonophores (colony jellyfish). For real! You could admire them floating across the 154-metre-long marble façade of the UN every evening.

As we've already seen, colony jellyfish are made up of individual animals, which come together to form something like a colony, or, better still, a nation. The individual animals then work together in a concerted effort to ensure the survival of all. So the whole creature is the sum of its individual animals. Basically, siphonophores do what the UN is trying to do: work

together for the good of all nations and people on this earth. And how are we doing? Well! Let me put it this way: the jellyfish certainly do it much better! And so even the UN finds these unique creatures, and I quote, "inspiring". "Inspiring jellyfish"— wouldn't that have been an excellent title for our book?

# The siphonophores. Can anyone even pronounce it?!

For starters, the siphonophores are free-swimming cnidarians that consist of anything from "many" to "very many" individual animals (there can be thousands of them). We have already met the "Portuguese man o'war", the most well-known (because it's also the most poisonous) representative of this jellyfish family. The individual animals that form these organisms are called polyps, another word we already know!

When I first heard about siphonophores, I found it astonishing that such "associations" also exist in the sea. Of course, on dry land, animal colonies are not unusual—just think of all the ant hills, wasps' nests or termite castles. Insects are frequently organized in colonies. They share their tasks and usually have a queen who keeps everything running smoothly. By the way, these are not democracies. They are all monarchies because

there is no insect colony without a queen (who takes care of reproduction)!

But did you know that there are also animal colonies underwater? That was entirely new for me!

## FOR BRIGHT MINDS

Only one mammalian species (apart from us humans) forms colonies with a precise distribution of tasks: the naked mole rat. You've never heard of naked mole rats? They are not exactly what we would call "pretty". They look a bit like mice without fur. Naked mole rats live in deep tunnel systems and belong to the rodent family. They are usually "ruled" by two queens, each giving birth to about sixty young per year. As a rule, about 300 of these animals form a naked mole rat colony. Some help raise the young, others build the tunnels, others guard the entrances and exits and defend them against snakes, for example. Some just carry soil out of the tunnels, and so on. The naked mole rat is a highly unusual animal. So please check them out (you can find them in lots of zoos)!

In any case, these jellyfish colonies drift happily through the sea. They are stronger and more organized together than a single polyp could ever be. The individuals in such colonies are also called "zooids", but you don't have to remember that. Unsurprisingly, in such a community, the individual members also take on different tasks. This means the individual polyps can look completely different, depending on their job. Some, for example, form a buoy or flotation bell (as in the Portuguese man o'war). They are responsible for keeping the colony afloat in the water. Other polyps are responsible for steering, others for food gathering, others for defence, and some for reproduction. Others just kind of "feel" around the environment, and so on. Some of these "zooids" also clone themselves because that is a more straightforward form of reproduction for them. This is very real—it's not a movie!

I should probably introduce you to some siphonophore species by name. And new ones are being discovered all the time. Recently, off Australia, researchers filmed a strange, spiralling USO in the water. The peculiar discs had a circumference of around forty-seven metres (!)—and at first, no one knew exactly what it was.

Everyone was stunned at the sight, according to biologists Nerida Wilson and Lisa Kirkendale from the Western

# Who can find the seven differences between the pictures? Solution: p.139

You have to pay close attention
in the ocean!

Australian Museum, who spoke to the science portal
ScienceAlert. People came running excitedly from all over
the ship to the look at the video screen. It eventually turned
out that the creature was a siphonophore, probably the largest known specimen of its kind to date. Presumably, a *Praya
dubia*. You can see some particularly stunning footage of
them in the documentary *Blue Planet II*, narrated by David
Attenborough.

Apropos (meaning "speaking of") films: jellyfish often serve
as a model for filmmakers when they portray aliens. Like in
the film *War of the Worlds* (2005) or *Arrival* (2016).

I could list page after page of artists (fashion designers, paint-
ers and so on) who have also been inspired by jellyfish. The
natural scientist Ernst Haeckel made beautiful jellyfish drawings as early as 1900, which Prince Albert of Monaco liked so
much that he commissioned a jellyfish chandelier 100 years
later. Some confectioners bake jellyfish cakes, submarine
designers want to make their vessels look like jellyfish, and
some researchers have even built soft robots inspired by jellyfish. What's weird is those robotic jellyfish can swim much
faster than the real ones. The researchers hope to be able to
pilot the animals to better explore the oceans.

Incidentally, in 2005, scientists caught some specimens of the siphonophore genus *Erenna* at a depth of around 2,000 metres. They noticed that their freshly formed tentacles emitted blue-green light, while fully grown tentacles emitted red light. Since then, researchers have speculated that the jellyfish could use the red light to attract various fish as prey in the deep sea. A remarkable video was once shot by a diving robot team from the oil industry, which filmed a creature hovering above the seabed at a depth of 1,325 metres off the West African coast. It looked more like some kind of spaghetti monster—and was later identified as a siphonophore: *Bathyphysa conifera*.

I personally find siphonophores to be even more mysterious than other medusae. We know less about them than you'd think—and most don't have English names either. So feel free to come up with some!

# FOR BRIGHT MINDS

I can't end this chapter without letting you know a few of the extraordinary and highly scientific Latin names of some siphonophore species. Do you think you could make up English names for them? (On page 134, you will find a link to some amazing siphonophore photos that will help you with this.)

(A) *Rhizophysa eysenhardtii* (B) *Bathyphysa conifera* (C) *Hippopodius hippopus* (D) *Kephyes hiulcus* (E) *Desmophyes haematogaster* (F) *Sphaeronectes christiansonae* (G) *Praya dubia* (H) *Apolemia* (I) *Lychnagalma utricularia* (J) *Nanomia* (K) *Physophora hydrostatica*. Phew, what a load of tongue-twisters! By the way, I call siphonophore (I) "shining deep-sea cactus". And (F) "glass dome with eagle flying away".

Finally, some siphonophore jellyfish can get really long, but do you know what the absolute longest animal in the world is? It lives in the sea and is known as *Lineus longissimus*. It is usually thirty metres long, but a sixty-metre-long specimen once washed up on a beach. That is about half the length of a football pitch! This animal is a type of ribbon worm.

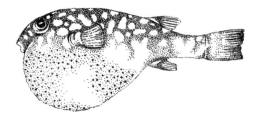

So do you want to try and come up with names for some of those weird siphonophore species above? I've left a little space here for that—let your imagination run wild.

CHAPTER
06

# WHICH TYPE OF JELLYFISH WOULD I BE?

Well, what can I say? You are spoilt for choice. There are countless species of jellyfish, and, at the risk of repeating myself, many of them are utterly unknown to us. New medusae are constantly being discovered. It's a bottomless pit because the oceans are so vast. Incidentally, the world-renowned jellyfish specialist Dr Gerhard Jarms once answered a question about how many species of jellyfish there are by saying: "it depends". First of all, what exactly is counted as a jellyfish. We already know that, professor! Comb jellies look like jellyfish, but they lack the characteristic cnidocysts. That is why zoologists do not classify them as medusae. Biologists would consider jellyfish to be all the "true jellyfish", "box jellyfish" and "hydromedusae". Just remember the Medusa 101 (from page 92) and our jellyfish classification from earlier.

All in all, according to the professor, there are about 930 known species. Others put the number at 2,000. However, it is thought there may be as many as 300,000 species of jellyfish in our seas. If this proves accurate, then there is still much to discover.

# Can you find all seven jellyfish hiding here?

Solution: p.142

But which of all the many jellyfish species best matches your personality? Of course, this is a silly question, but let's have a go at answering it… (Illustrations on page 120.)

1.	Type 1: Are you easy to pick out of a crowd? Do you like to eat mushrooms and help in the kitchen? Are you good-natured and do you hate to hurt anyone? Are you a good swimmer, fairly tall and would you like to travel from Brazil to Japan?

	Then I'd say you're in good hands with the cannonball jellyfish (*Stomolophus meleagris*). This medusa looks like a mushroom and is also one of the species used in cooking (mainly in Asia). It is an active swimmer, grows up to twenty-five centimetres and is found from New England to Brazil, Southern California, Ecuador, the Sea of Japan and the South China Sea. Stings by this jellyfish are painful but rarely fatal.

2.	Type 2: Are in a foul mood every morning? Do you wake up with a toxic look on your face? Do people tend to stay away from you until lunchtime? Do you explode when someone speaks to you or dares to touch you?

If so, then I'd say you're more of a box jellyfish type. The sea wasp (*Chironex fleckeri*) was already mentioned in the list of Australia's poisonous animals. Sea wasps have sixty tentacles, each with 500,000 toxic spines, and a sting is so painful that many people stung by them suffer shock and drown. It's best not to get too close to these medusae; of course, it would be madness to keep them in an aquarium.

3. Type 3: Perhaps you're more of the leisurely type? Do you like hanging out with people? Do you like the North Sea and Baltic beaches? Maybe you wouldn't hurt a fly and love a cuddle?

Oh, how nice, then you are clearly a kindred spirit to the moon jellyfish with the scientific name *Aurelia aurita*. It sounds quite lovely, and you'd probably knock on any door with that name on it. These medusae are utterly harmless to humans. They float lazily with the currents and can be found in large numbers in the North and Baltic Seas. Sometimes they multiply rapidly, which is, of course, the fault of us humans who dump fertilizer in the sea (we over-fertilize our fields and it ends up being washed into rivers, then the sea). Jellyfish like fertilizer because it makes populations of their food, plankton, explode.

4. Type 4: Do you like fried eggs? That's all I need to know because if you said "yes" you'll love the fried-egg jellyfish. It looks like it's wearing a fried egg on its head. It can be found in the Mediterranean Sea, but you must be careful because it's not as harmless as an egg. It does protect small fish, though, allowing them to hide between its tentacles. They are immune to the jellyfish's poison.

5. Type 5: Do you love haunted castles? Do you like to throw a sheet over yourself and scare people? Would you prefer to be see-through and inconspicuous in the swimming pool? In that case you could team up with the ghost jellyfish (*Cyanea nozakii*). They have quite a potent venom that causes skin blisters and irritation. Fishermen don't like ghost jellyfish at all because they often clog their nets. Ghost jellyfish also like to feed on other jellyfish, which is thought to be one of the reasons edible jellyfish (which often end up on plates in Asia) are becoming less and less common. Or maybe humans are just fishing too many edible jellyfish out of the oceans?

6. Type 6: Did I hear you say there's a walnut tree in your family's garden? And you like walnut ice cream? And love chocolate nut cake? Do you have shoulder-length

hair and like bright colours? Oh really? Then you should get yourself a "sea walnut" (*Mnemiopsis leidyi*). It'll be perfect for you. This is a type of comb jellyfish, so it looks like a jellyfish, but strictly speaking, it isn't (dachshund cat!). Its body consists of transparent tissue with luminous lobes resembling ribs.

We could go on like this forever, but it would be easier for you to go in search of other species of medusae yourself. Perhaps you can take a closer look at any jellyfish you find washed up on the beach in the future? But don't touch them! Take a photo instead. And who knows, maybe you will be the scientist who discovers a whole new species of jellyfish? Then you'd better think of a good name, because you'll be able to name it yourself—maybe the new species will even be named after you? It's not uncommon for that to happen. Do you want an example? It won't take me long to find some!

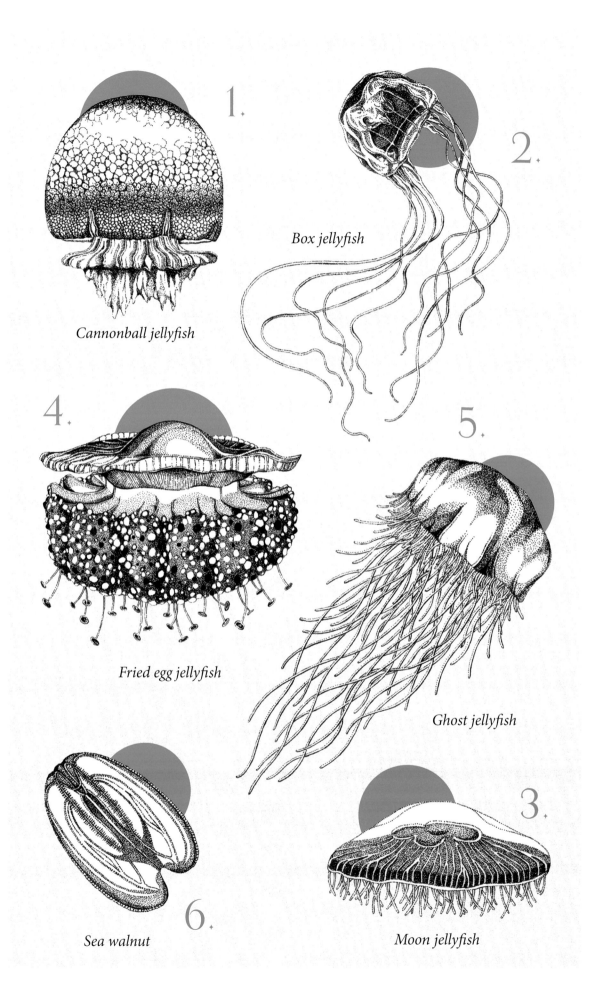

1. Cannonball jellyfish

2. Box jellyfish

4. Fried egg jellyfish

5. Ghost jellyfish

6. Sea walnut

3. Moon jellyfish

# The thing about names

Let's look at the *Bazinga rieki*, for example, a tiny jellyfish species that belongs to the true jellyfish. Root-mouth jellyfish are also often called marigold jellyfish because some parts of their bodies are curled like marigolds. A unique feature of these medusae is that they not only have a mouth in the middle of their body (like all other jellyfish) but also have mouths in each of their arm-like limbs.

Anyway, this medusa was discovered in 2011 by a certain Denis Riek on the east coast of Australia. It is a tiny, stout-looking jellyfish with a diameter of about two centimetres. It is also the only species in the "*Bazinga*" genus.

The genus "*Bazinga*" goes back to the sitcom *The Big Bang Theory*. There, "Bazinga" is an expression the character Dr Sheldon Cooper likes to use when he is making a fool of someone, and thus means something like "got you". This fitted perfectly, as *Bazinga rieki* was previously thought to be a juvenile of another, larger genera due to its small size. Thus it "fooled" the experts for a long time. A bazinga is also a type a musical instrument, namely a seven-stringed harp. The channels inside the medusa's umbrella reminded scientists of bazinga strings.

So let me recap: the jellyfish's "surname" (*rieki*) comes from the human discoverer and the "first name" (*Bazinga*) from a successful TV series. And they were also reminded of a harp when they saw it. Isn't that neat?

Even bacteria are sometimes named after scientists, such as the bacterium *Escherichia coli* (named after its discoverer Theodor Escherich). In 2021, a 15-million-year-old (and long extinct) snail species was named after the city of Vienna—the *Mitrella viennensis*. Its shells had been discovered stored in the basement of the Natural History Museum in Vienna. By the way, the German name for these animals is *Täubchenschnecke*: pigeon snail. Pretty, isn't it? Well, that's how naming works! And not only for animals, of course.

I'm sure you all know that, according to the school textbooks, a certain Christopher Columbus "discovered" America (which also marked the beginning of a horror story for the indigenous population). However, the name "America" comes from another adventurer, the Italian navigator Amerigo Vespucci. Christopher got there earlier, but Amerigo realized he was landing on a new continent, unlike Columbus, who was convinced he had found a new route to Asia. And that is why the continent was called America for the first time on a map in 1507. After Amerigo—voilà!

But let's stay with animals for a while—people like to name them after celebrities. Do you know what a "celebrity" is?

The kind of people who are on TV a lot, and everyone knows them. So, for example, there are two giant crab spiders called *Heteropoda ninahagen* and *Heteropoda davidbowie*, a sea snail called *Bursina borisbeckeri*, a species of ground beetle called *Agra schwarzeneggeri* —and even a dinosaur named Elvisaurus! Can you spot the celebrities hidden in their names? And if these people don't mean anything to you, don't worry! I'll just try some other animals.

American scientists have recently named four newly discovered species of darter fish after Barack Obama, Jimmy Carter, Teddy Roosevelt and Bill Clinton. Can you tell me what they all had in common? There is also an Australian horsefly named after Beyoncé, and a species of wasp called Frodo, Bilbo and Gandalf… do those names "ring" any bells?

And finally, some proper scientific guidance: when naming new animals, the scientific name must be written in Latin, with the suffix "*-ensis*" or the genitive forms "*-i*" or "*-ae*" added to any names. For example, if I had discovered the *Bazinga rieki*, it could have been called *Medusa stavarici* or *Medusa michaelensis*.

Grab your pencils... this picture is crying out
for a bit of colour. Do you dare?

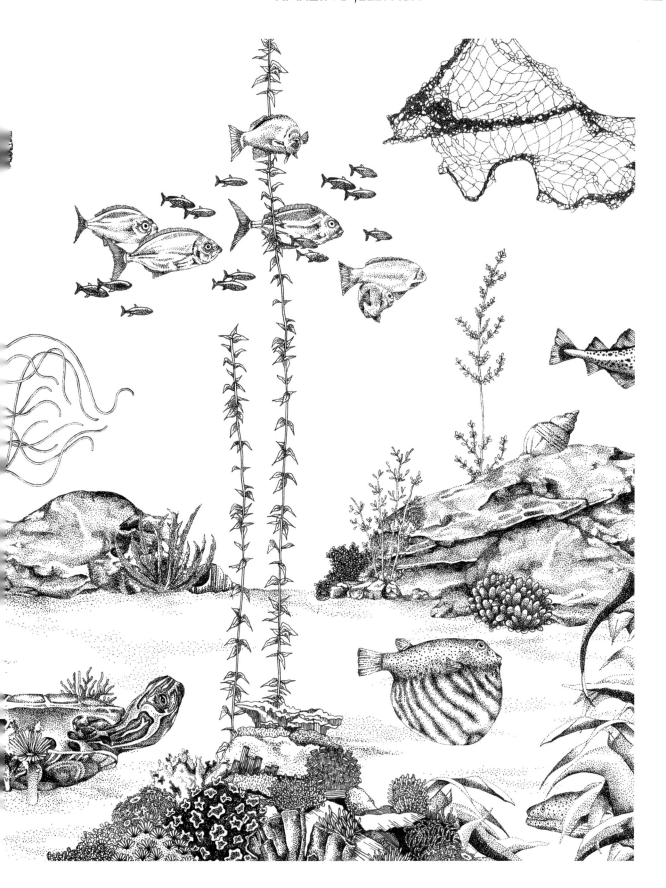

CHAPTER

07

# JELLYFISH FOR BEGINNERS
## (AND MODERATELY ADVANCED SPEAKERS)

Jellyfish is not too difficult a language. Anyone willing to put in a little effort can learn a few words straight away. And, as you know from school, language learning always starts with vocabulary! So let's create a first vocabulary book for Jellyfish. And I promise you, you'll soon be writing down a lot of words you've "discovered" yourself… After all, Jellyfish is not rocket science!

### Jellopatra *(n)*
We're of course talking about the famous queen of Egypt, Cleopatra, probably one of the most well-known women in world history. To this day, we have no idea where her grave is. Maybe being an archaeologist wouldn't be a bad job either?

### Jelldemort *(n)*
Is of course the jellyfish name for Lord Voldemort from the Harry Potter stories. Although naturally he's actually called Jelly Jotter, or something like that.

### Jellynese Waltz *(n)*
This is a very popular dance in Vienna, but not only there. Medusae can dance very well—take a close look next time you go to the aquarium. You might want to learn the waltz, too!

**Jellombia** *(n)*… Eh?

That is, Colombia in human languages. I'm already getting the hang of this Jellyfish thing. Anyway, Colombia is a country located at the northern edge of South America. A lot of jellyfish live there—in the ocean off the coast of Jellombia, of course.

**Potjellto** *(n)*

The potato is part of many delicious meals. Jellyfish—not so much. Well, in Asia some species are considered delicacies. The Japanese even make sweet treats out of them. The animals themselves won't make you put on any weight. But potjelltos will—especially as fries! That reminds me of a story about Danish researchers who are trying to create potato chips from jellyfish. They're making progress, so who knows, maybe you'll find them soon on a supermarket shelf near you?

**Jauls** *(n)*

Jauls are a very well-known comic-book people. The main characters are Astjellix and Objellix. They have a dog called Jellmatix. Have you figured out who I'm talking about? They are all very brave. The only thing they're afraid of is that the sky will fall down on them. I'm more afraid of the ceiling coming down on me… but that's another story.

**Jellator** *(n)*

Hm, maybe Jellyfish isn't quite as easy as I first thought. What could this mean, I wonder? Well, on our planet, this thing is about forty thousand kilometres long, but it's really only an imaginary line that splits our planet in half. Do the countries Jellermany or Monjellya lie on the equator? You'd have to check a jetlas.

## Jelladpole *(n)*

We call them tadpoles. As a kid I used to fish them out of ponds and then watch in amazement as they turned into frogs.

## Jellendar *(n)*

I need this more than anyone. Without a jellendar I'm completely lost. I usually don't even know which day of the week it is. But don't tell anyone. Please?

## Jing-Jong

…is definitely a jorilla, probably the most famous of them all. A lot of movies have been made about him. You've probably seen some on TV or in the cinema. More recently, he's even been fighting dinosaurs. He likes to climb up very tall buildings. Know who I'm talking about?

## Jallinka *(n)*

OK, this one is a bit more difficult. The translation is "*Kalinka*". This is the title of one of the more well-known Russian folk songs. Kalinka is the diminutive (as in cutesy) form of "Kalina" which is the berry of the highbush cranberry (*Viburnum opulus*). It's also known as the European cranberry. The song goes: Калинка, калинка, калинка моя! В саду ягода малинка, малинка моя! Sorry—that was Russian. They use what is called the Cyrillic alphabet. "*Kalinka, kalinka, kalinka moya! V sadu yagoda malinka, malinka moya!*"—at least that makes it look a little more recognizable. But what does it mean? Let me try to translate: "Snowberry, snowberry, snowberry of mine. The berry in the garden, the raspberry is mine." It's a bummer you can't hear the melody now. I'm injellatuated, I mean infatuated with this song.

# SEE YOU SOON, MY FRIENDS!

Wasn't this a cool trip we took to the world of the jellyfish? I learnt so much myself, I guess that's why I like writing books! And if we ever meet somewhere, we can now confidently speak "Jellyfish" to each other. Practise it with your parents!

In the meantime, I'm thinking about which animal species to take a closer look at next. What makes sense after all the octopuses and jellyfish? Feel free to send suggestions to the publisher (you'll find the address in the book). And maybe you'll send us some particularly beautiful jellyfish drawings. We'll put them on our website with your name—and I'll post them on Instagram myself!

# YOU WANT TO KNOW MORE?

We've put together some links. This is of course just a small selection. Check these out, then go find some more stuff about jellyfish!

✦ **Weight-on-the-moon-calculator:**

http://www.learningaboutelectronics.com/Articles/Weight-on-the-moon-conversion-calculator.php

✦ **The Great Pacific Garbage Patch:**

https://education.national-geographic.org/resource/great-pacific-garbage-patch/

✦ **Microplastics on the seabed:**

https://www.theguardian.com/environment/2020/apr/30/microplastics-found-in-greater-quantities-than-ever-before-on-sea-bed-currents-hotspots

✦ **Stinging nettles:**

https://www.bbc.com/future/article/20220518-why-you-should-embrace-stinging-nettles

✦ **How to draw a jellyfish:**

https://www.youtube.com/watch?v=KfGToUpNItg

✦ **Native butterflies:**
*…use this link for Britain:*

https://www.wildlifetrusts.org/wildlife/identify-british-butterflies

*…use this link for North America:*

https://www.butterfliesandmoths.org/identify/region/united-states

✦ **Humans can live to 150 years old:**

https://www.scientificamerican.com/article/humans-could-live-up-to-150-years-new-research-suggests/

✦ **The biggest aquarium in Europe:**

https://de.nordsoenoceanarium.dk/

✦ **The world of jellyfish—documentaries:**

https://www.documentarytube.com/best-of/the-best-documentaries-about-jellyfish/

✦ **Colony jellyfish (siphonophores):**

https://commons.wikimedia.org/wiki/File:Photographs_of_living_siphonophores.jpg

Copyright © Minitta Kandlbauer

Michael Stavaric, born 1972 in Brno, lives as a freelance writer, translator and lecturer in Vienna. He would have liked to become a marine biologist. Now he writes children's books, novels, plays and poems, but is still interested in animals and plants, especially marine animals.

Copyright © Michèle Ganser

Michèle Ganser, born in Aachen in 1995, studied communication design in Aachen and Mainz. She is particularly fascinated by the universe, the stars and the different planets. In her illustrations she combines exciting themes in an unusual way and thus creates completely new worlds. In her free time she likes to read—preferably science-fiction novels.

**Weight on the Moon and Sun…**

On the Moon: 33.0682977 kilograms
On the Sun: 5,600 kilograms, or 5.6 tonnes (wow!)

**Solutions to page 38**

1. Rays sting. They have a poisonous sting on their tail, which can be really dangerous.

2. With the horsefly it's quite clear, and allow me to make it abundantly clear, these little vermin bite, so they don't sting.

3. Of course, the hedgehog stings in defence. But does it bite? Let's say, theoretically. It has teeth, but it would never really bite us.

4. The platypus actually stings. It has a poisonous spur, which is more or less a bigger sting.

5. If you look at a picture of the thorny devil, it is obvious that it stings. By the way, its thorns also collect dew, which is handy in the desert when you're thirsty.

6. Everything is true for ants; it just depends on the type of ant. Some bite, others just sting, some bite and sting, the whole package!

7. Of course, the puffer fish also mainly stings (and its poison is very dangerous). But it also bites if you put your finger in its mouth.

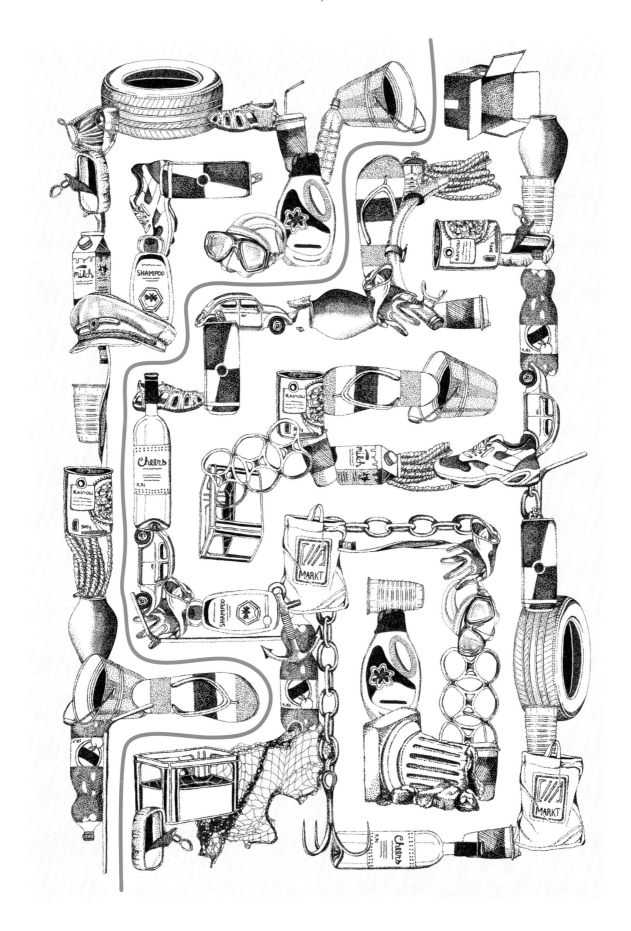

So much plastic... find the way through!

Image: p.17

# Help the jellyfish find the right food!

Image: p.80

# Who can find the seven differences between the pictures?

Image: p.106

Can you find all seven things that
do not belong in the sea? Image: p.24

# Can you find all seven jellyfish hiding here?

Image: p.114

Pushkin Press
Somerset House, Strand
London WC2R 1LA

*Amazing Jellyfish* was first published as *Faszination Qualle* by Leykam
Buchverlagsgesellschaft m.b.H. Nfg. & Co. KG, in Graz – Vienna, Austria, 2023

First published by Pushkin Press in 2024

9 8 7 6 5 4 3 2 1

ISBN 13: 978-1-78269-425-0

≡ Federal Ministry
Republic of Austria
Arts, Culture,
Civil Service and Sport

Typeset by Tetragon, London
Printed and bound in China by C&C Offset Printing Co Ltd.

www.pushkinpress.com